Selling Homes 1-2-3

Insider Advice on Becoming

A Surprisingly Better

Part-time or Full-time

Real Estate Agent

Bob Boog

THS INTERNATIONAL

SELLING HOMES 1-2-3

Insider Advice on Becoming
A Surprisingly Better Part-time or Full-time
Real Estate Agent

By Bob Boog
Editor: Robin Quinn
Cover Art Design by Bob Boog
and Crest Typographers, Valencia, California

THS International
Post Office Box 221283
Santa Clarita, CA. USA 91322-1283

Library of Congress Catalog Card Number: 98-96509

ISBN No: 0-9666130-1-5
First Printing 1998
Printed in the United States of America

MONEY-BACK GUARANTEE: If you are not completely
satisfied with this book you may return it for a full refund
within ten days of purchase. Books must be shipped
unmarked and accompanied with a copy of the purchaser's
receipt.

THS International
PUBLISHING HOUSE

Acknowledgements

To all my past and present clients, friends and competitors, thank you.

To my mother and father, Joan and Paul Boog, who supported me in everything I've ever tried, I love you.

To my wife, Roxana Boog, thank you for putting up with me for the last 14 years. I love you more than I can say.

To my sons: Brandon who likes my stories, and Kevin who likes my drawings, you guys are everything to me.

To my mother-in-law, Clemencia Palomo, thank you for putting up with me and watching the boys. You're terrific.

To Robin Quinn, my editor, thank you for your attention to detail and cheerleading on the sidelines.

To Burt Hicks, thank you for reading my manuscript. Your humorous asides were appreciated! Thanks also to Mike and Sandy Sorenson, BJ and Jeannie Atkins, Kevin and Leslie Wessell and Lou and Kathy Fritz for friendship and good company.

To John Hess and Susan Vann, thank you. You're an inspiration to us all.

Thank you to my eight brothers and sisters: Pat, Kevin,Tom, Sean and Rosie Boog, and Jackie Kipka, Paula Wright and Margo Heller who taught me negotiating skills at an early age. Thanks also to my six in-laws: Leon and Sandy Frommer, Isabel and Ryan Hellerud, Patty and Tomas Velazquez, who have helped me to retain those skills today.

Thanks to my real estate colleagues for making me a better agent: Jerry Fischkes, Glenn Stuart, Mike Moeller, Dean Damron, Robert Danaian and Jim Behan.

To Dan Poynter, thank you for helping me accomplish my goal of publishing my book. To Crest Typographers in Valencia, thank you Joyce, Cheri and Vicki.

Finally, thank you to Tom Hopkins, Mike Ferry and Barb Schwarz. You opened my eyes to selling homes more professionally.

Disclaimer

This book is designed to provide information in regard to the subject of selling homes. It is sold with the understanding that the publisher and author are not engaged in rendering legal, accounting or other professional services. If legal or other expert assistance is required, the services of a competent professional should be sought.

It is not the purpose of this book to print all the information that is available on the subject of selling homes, but to complement, amplify and supplement other texts. You are urged to read all the available books on selling homes that are available and to tailor the information to your specific needs.

The techniques, ideas and procedures found in Selling Homes One-Two-Three are tools which many agents can use to become surprisingly better in their real estate careers. However these tools are not intended to be misused.

Although efforts have been made to make this book as complete and accurate as possible, there may be mistakes made in content and typography. What may be an acceptable practice in one state may not be acceptable in another. Therefore, this text should be used as only a general guide and not as the ultimate source of information. Agents are hereby advised to follow the laws and regulations of state and local governments as well as their real estate board.

The purpose of this book is to educate and entertain. The author and THS International shall have neither liability nor responsibility to any person or entity with respect to any loss or damage caused, or alleged to be caused, directly or indirectly by the information contained in this book.

Table of Contents

Warning

There was once a beautiful woman who didn't speak English very well. She was visiting Chicago for the first time and when she left a movie theater by herself late one summer night, she needed to know what time it was. So she approached a man who was standing alone at a street corner to ask him the time.

She walked right up to him and asked in her broken English: "Do you have time?"

The man looked back at her, surprised. Then he answered: "Sure. What did you have in mind?

I mention this story because sometimes just **one word** makes all the difference in the world. Now, if the woman had asked, "Do you have **the** time?" the man might have responded, "Yes. It's 9:30." She might have gotten a completely different answer to her question.

Likewise, it's often the *little things* that can make a big difference in selling real estate. But sometimes we don't realize their importance. In this book I want to talk about some of these little details: words, concepts and ideas, that you probably won't find in any of the other real estate sales books available. By doing these little things, however, you can become a surprisingly better real estate agent!

My goal is to bridge the gap of information that I think exists for some full-time agents, people new to real estate and part-time agents. In this book, I'm going to share with you some of my insider secrets that I've learned from selling real estate for the past twenty years. Even if you aren't interested in selling homes for a living I still think that you will enjoy reading this book and telling friends about it.

Warning: Because I'm concentrating on subjects not found in other books, you're **not** going to find chapters on setting goals, time management, making a business plan and asking questions. Those topics are important, however, **so if you do need help in those areas, please refer to the Reading and Listening Resources found on page 183 of this book.**

Now, if you are brand new to real estate, I recommend that you purchase a 3-ring binder and divide it into six sections. The headings of these sections are as follows:

1) Office rules and policies: Here's where you'll put information about the office. How to enter names into your database. A list of the pager numbers of other agents. How to update your electronic keypad. How to submit an e-mail complaint to HUD. Get answers to all the "how do we do this?" questions and keep them here. Learn to become self-sufficient.

2) Purchase contract samples: Keep copies of properly filled-out purchase agreements. Type them so that they are legible. Include any and all disclosures such as transfer, agency and lead-based paint disclosures and keep them in this section.

3) Photo-brochures of homes you've previewed: Save some photo-brochures of homes you've seen on tour. Make notes on the pages to help job your memory, "cute home with yucky orange carpet." Notes like this will help keep the inventory of homes you see sorted in your mind.

4) Financing Information: Store information on interest rates, points and loan fees in this file. Include estimated closing cost sheets and monthly payments for VA and FHA loans along with conventional and jumbo loans. Also have a copy of a settlement statement from an escrow or title company and several credit authorization forms.

5) Referral directory: Work without leaving home by having the names and phone numbers of escrow companies, lawyers, title companies, loan reps in this section. It's wise to save this info on computer disk if possible, as people in this industry do tend to switch companies. Also it's handy to have a list of utilities: electric, gas, telephone, and cable. Also have names of handy-men, painters, and carpet-layers.

6) Ideas on selling: This is where you keep seminar notes, news clippings, flyers from the competition, etc. Collecting sales tips will soon become your hobby! Spend an hour each night studying books and listening to tapes on selling. In no time at all, you'll become an expert!

In addition, purchase the kind of 3-ring binder with pocket folders. Use these pockets to save small receipts, or write **SMALL RECEIPTS** on a 9 x 12 clasp envelope. Once a month you'll empty this envelope and record your postage receipts, gas receipts, etc. in Quickbooks or other tax-related software for tax purposes.

Now, some of you may **not** be new to real estate. Some of you may have worked in real estate for many years, others may have only worked part-time, but whatever your level of experience, I imagine that you do enjoy being paid. Being paid to show and sell real estate. Ah, what compares with it? Depositing an escrow check into a checking or savings account is on of the most enjoyable experiences in real estate, isn't it? (Say yes.)

My hope is that after finishing these pages you will come to understand how to better handle clients in order to make a few more sales each and every year, but whether or not you make any more sales is strictly up to you. You must decide what level of performance you want to expect from yourself. The fact that you are reading this book shows me that you're dedicated and want to improve.

Feel free to make notes in the margins, highlight text, and if you get the urge, send me your comments and critiques.

Now before we get started, let me explain **why** I wrote this book.

Why I Wrote This Book

A friend of mine speculated that my motive for writing this book was to get rich. And I'd be lying to you if I didn't admit that one of the reasons for writing it was to make lots of money. Because like most everybody else I want to make a few dollars.

Somebody else said that I probably wrote this book because I'm sick and tired of selling real estate and want to get the heck out of it. (Not true.)

I'm still having fun selling homes. What's exciting now is that I'm selling homes to some of the sons and daughters of my past clients!

Actually, I also wrote this book because I wanted to inspire and encourage real estate agents to do better. Not only do I want them to become better salespeople for the sake of their own clients but for other people too.

I recently had a bad experience with a young, top producer in my area, and it bothered me so much that I decided to put pen to paper. I felt that I needed to say something because the **loan officer handling the transaction told me that 90% of real estate agents working nowadays would have done the same thing as this top agent.**

Now before I get on my high horse, I want you to know that I wouldn't still be selling real estate today if it weren't for the hundreds and maybe thousands of good people that I've met over the years. Good clients, good prospects, good real estate associates, and tough, but good competitors. The reason for my success is because I've been blessed to work with so many good people.

Recently though I felt embarrassed to be in real estate. Here's what happened. My buyer was a young man, age 36, who has been paralyzed from the waist down for the last ten years. Divorced, he's sharing the responsibility of raising his eleven year-old daughter. He works as a professional fisherman and drives a specially-designed vehicle to pull his boat.

He wanted to buy a home that had a garage big enough to house his bass boat, and spacious bathroom entrances and wide hallways, to make it easy for him to get around in his wheelchair. In my area, these kinds of homes are fairly difficult to find in his price range.

My client fell in love with a home that was owned and listed by a young, top agent and wrote up a purchase agreement that was slightly less than full price. When I visited the agent to discuss my client's offer, he looked at the buyer's pre-approval letter, he listened to me tell him how much my wheelchair-bound client liked his home and then he faxed me a strange counteroffer which he didn't bother to sign. Number one: *he asked my buyer to release an earnest money deposit of $2,500 unconditionally to him within two days.* Number two: *my buyer was supposed to close escrow within one week or he would lose his deposit.* Now this wasn't a loan assumption. My buyer was supposed to obtain and qualify for a new loan and close escrow within seven days. Not a normal counteroffer, wouldn't you agree?

My buyer still wanted the home, so the next day he met with a loan officer. Afterwards the loan officer told me that he could complete the sale in one week. Upon hearing this news, the listing agent said, "I'm sorry, but I just received another offer. It's from another agent, and the price is slightly higher than yours, so I'm taking it."

Now, did the listing agent use our offer as leverage to gain a higher price from the second buyer? I don't want to speculate, but doesn't it seem that way? It was almost as if he didn't want my purchaser to buy this property and it made me shake my head in disgust. It wasn't the fact that I lost the commission. It was the fact that meanness had triumphed again. My buyer was willing to do anything to get that home, only to have his hopes dashed. I mean it takes him one hour just to put his pants on in the morning and he met the loan officer at seven o'clock in the morning. Yet by eight o'clock that same morning, the top agent had received and accepted this other offer.

Another disappointment in a life filled with disappointments. My client felt bad too.

I realize that we Realtors® live in a rough and tumble world and that rejection and disappointment are part of the game. And perhaps it was best that he didn't get this house. That's what I told him. "Hey, things will work out for the best." Still I kept saying to myself, legally this top agent has the right to break his promise to sell the home, but I don't think that it's right, or that it promotes a good image of what real estate agents are normally like.

Question: How could I turn this negative experience into a positive one?

I started to think about what the lender had said; "Ninety percent of real estate agents would have done the same thing." But I don't think this is true. Most agents would have written a counteroffer notifying each purchaser that there was another purchaser interested in the property. Most agents are considerate and don't play games. Then the listing agent told me, "Bob, just shove it under the rug and move on. *There's nothing you can do about it.*" I guess he was right. I guess I should have just swept it under the rug.

But see, I'm the dumb kind of agent.

I figured that maybe I could do something about it. See I had started working on this book but I'd stopped writing. Suddenly I got inspired to finish it. Why not mention this incident? If nothing else, maybe new or part-time agents could learn something and become surprisingly better agents as a result.

But who am I to write a book? Who would want to read it?

That's why I'd stopped writing it in the first place. I'd said to myself, Who am I kidding? I can't razzle-dazzle people with my sales achievements. How I sold seventeen homes with one hand tied behind my back, that kind of thing, because even when I had a good year there was always somebody else who did even better.

One time I went to a Mike Ferry seminar and he had everybody raise their hands in order to see who had made the most sales.

To my surprise, I was the number one salesperson in the room of three hundred people.

So Mike walked over to me and he asked, "What's your name?"

I said, "Bob."

He said, "Bob, do you realize that there's a guy in Michigan who sold almost three times as many homes as you did last year?"

The point is, no matter how good you think you're doing, there's probably somebody, somewhere else, who's doing it better. Then I realized that I've probably failed and gotten up from the floor more than the next person, so what the heck. Maybe I should write about my failures as well as my successes. So here are three reasons why I wrote this book.

One: I want to make lots of money.

Two: I want to teach you something about working with buyers. I work in Newhall, California where I managed to sell 29 homes in sixteen weeks after the 1994 Northridge earthquake, during a time when selling homes was probably much more difficult than it is today. I'm going to share with you some of my winning secrets and losing experiences. In fact, you might learn more from my failures than my secrets. I don't know.

Three: I want you to learn that selling homes isn't only about making the most money. I think it's more important to lose a sale if it means doing the right thing. Who wants to be number-one, if, like the young agent in my town, you stomp the hopes of somebody less fortunate in order to make a few more dollars? (To see the procedure that Bob uses for multiple offers, see page 100.)

When I was brand new in real estate, there was a real estate broker who had a heart attack. Every realtor in town went out of their way to help him out. Nowadays many of us wouldn't even bother to send a "get well soon" card.

I think that we in real estate can do a little bit better than we're doing. For our sellers, buyers and even our competitors.

So I'm going on my own little crusade. I don't know if there is anyone out there who feels like I do, but I think it's best if we all start doing something. For example, why not start by making some random acts of appreciation. Say nice things to people, or send notes, or e-mail, not only to buyers and sellers, but other agents as well. Believe me, many are starved for praise and appreciation. And just a few words is all it takes. *"Thanks for your professionalism on Ermine Street."* Give a person doing a good job some honest encouragement.

You might be amazed at the results!

Okay, now that I've got that matter off my chest, let's get started!

CHAPTER ONE
Orientation

Somebody once humorously defined a real estate agent as: "...a courageous individual who insists on believing that he can support himself and his family by trying to sell that which nobody can afford to buy."

It's a well-established fact that most new full-time and part-time agents are taught that the key to making money in real estate is to get *listings*. But most agents are quick to discover that getting listings is not that easy and they end up leaving the business. Most are lucky to break even after paying for their board fees, business cards, advertising and promotional materials. Many new agents leave real estate without ever making a single sale. Why?

This may shake the traditional real estate tree of wisdom, but I think the problem is that we brokers don't try very hard to teach new agents or part-time agents how to work with **buyers**. Instead we want agents out of the office, prospecting and getting listings. Yet many sellers are reluctant to list their home with a new or part-time agent. Often a seller will interview more than one agent, and if they ask to see a track record of satisfied clients, or recent television ads or newspaper promotions, it puts the new or part-time agent at a disadvantage.

Yet believe it or not, many top listing agents have started out their real estate careers by working with buyers. Along the way, these agents picked up useful information and techniques that they later used to transition themselves to working more with sellers. By first working with buyers, they became surprisingly better at selling themselves to sellers. You can too.

So before we go any further, I want to make it clear that **the objective of this book is to help you become surprisingly better at working with buyers.**

Now in this chapter, I want to start by answering three questions that are frequently asked by new or part-time agents, and then we'll talk about a secret that most successful agents have discovered. Perhaps you already know it.

Question #1: "What's the difference between a buyer's agent and any other real estate agent?"

All across the United States, there are different definitions of buyer's agents. In most states, a buyer's agent has a written contract with the buyer, much like a listing agent has a contract with a seller. A buyer-broker agreement or buyer listing says that the agent is working solely for the buyer.

Note: You have to follow the rules that are set up for you in your state, but for this book I want you to know that I'm going to consider **any person** with a valid real estate license, who represents a buyer in a real estate transaction, to be a buyer's agent. So if you have thirty listings and like to work with three or four buyers, that's fine with me. If you don't have a written buyer-broker agreement, that's okay, you're still a buyer's agent. I'm making up the rules here, okay? In other words, whenever you are working to represent buyers, you are considered to be a buyer's agent or a selling agent. (In this book, selling agent, and buyer's agent may be used interchangeably.)

Question #2: "What about getting listings?"

Floyd Wickman once said that getting listings is the name of the game in real estate. What do I think about that? Isn't getting listings more important than working with buyers?

Getting listings is not the focus of this book and I don't want to spend a whole lot of time on this well-traveled subject.

Instead, I'm going to assume that one of these statements represents a goal that you'd like to achieve: "I want to become a better buyer's agent," or "I want to sell more homes to buyers."

Why have this be your goal? Let's be honest with ourselves. Not everyone can be the star quarterback. Not everyone can be the top listing agent in town. Not everyone can handle the stress of making ten listings one month and selling fifteen homes the following month. But the average person could use a few tips on working with buyers, I'm hoping that this book will be of help to you.

Question #3: "Why do I think that buyer's agents are still going to be around for the next twenty years?"

There are a lot of agents who are afraid that the Internet, cable television, Costco, Prudential or Random House will take over the real estate industry and throw realtors out on the street. In the future, with a virtual reality headset on, a buyer wouldn't even need a realtor. Right? What makes me think that real estate agents are even going to be around five to ten years from now?

If you're kind of a skeptical person, you're probably going to like this answer because it goes: **Things in real estate aren't always the way they seem to be**. Let me illustrate this point with a little story.

I had a buyer come to my office who had already found a house he wanted to buy and he asked me to just write up the purchase agreement. He said, "Bob, the seller is selling it 'by owner' and he said he'll pay any agent I select a four percent commission. Can you live with that?"

I thought to myself, **Can I live with that? Alleluia! Today is my lucky day! I don't even have to show the freakin' house!** But to my buyer, I looked thoughtful as I uttered: "For you? No problem." Then I hurried to write up the paperwork. However, when the buyer told me that the home wasn't connected to the public water system, I stopped writing. "If the place has a well, you should have a well certification done," I suggested.

The buyer told me, "No, don't worry about it. The seller just got the well certified last week. He gave me a copy of the certification, too. He said, "The well man says that it pumped for eighteen hours at 1.75 gallons a minute and that the well is fantastic."

"That sounds great," I said, "But can you fax me a copy of it for my records?"

When I got the faxed copy, the information was just as he had told me. The report was only a week old and it stated that the well had pumped 1.75 gallons a minute for 18 hours.

So I called up the man who did the well test. I said, "Hi, my name is Bob and I'm calling to ask you a couple of questions about the well report that you did over on Carson Street."

The well digger was a crotchety old soul. He said, "What's

the matter with you, son? You say you've got the report. Can't you read?"

I said, "Reading isn't the problem, sir. In the report you stated that you pumped the well for eighteen hours and it produced 1.75 gallons a minute. Is that right?"

He said, "Yes, that sounds about right."

I said, "Well, is that good or bad?"

He said, "What do you mean?"

I said, "I'm sorry sir, but I'm probably the dumbest agent in town. I don't know how to interpret the information. So tell me, is this a good well or a bad well?"

He said, "You guys are all the same. Of course it's bad. That's what I told the seller. I told him he needs to dig a new

Is this a good well...  Or a Bad Well?

well. There are four parties drawing off that well. The copy of the well-share agreement is right there, isn't it?"

Like I said, things aren't always the way they seem to be.

Most people new to the real estate business think it's a piece of cake. All we real estate people do is wait for the phone to ring, drive a buyer to see a house and then collect an enormous commission, right? *But things aren't always the way they seem to be, are they?*

Why do buyers and sellers pay us a fee? We get paid to make certain that all the details of a real estate transaction are taken care of while our clients attend to the details of their lives. Who wants to have a well not work six weeks after moving into a place? Whom would the buyer blame if it didn't work?

Buyers want somebody to watch out for their interests because they've got their own jobs and lives to live. I once got a FISBO (For-Sale-By-Owner) listing because the owner spent so much time talking to the buyer's lender on the phone while at her job that she almost got fired. When the sale fell out, she didn't want to go through that experience again. Most buyers and sellers are the same. They want to sleep easily at night reassured that there is somebody protecting their interests so that things will turn out like they want.

Sometimes we have to work our butts off to make sure that this happens, too, don't we?

Because in real life, escrows don't always close on time. People are people. Things aren't always the way they seem to be, so a good attitude to have is "don't believe everything that people tell you." **Get it in writing.**

Buyers are liars and sellers never tell the truth. Right?

Having this kind of skeptical attitude helps explain why a good buyer's agent usually brings information on two or three "switch" properties when the buyer says, "I only have time to see one home." Because many times a purchaser **does** have time to look and will write up a purchase agreement after seeing the second or third home. The skeptical or prepared agent wins. The gullible or unprepared agent loses.

To be honest, many buyers may have ten solid reasons for being cagey. They may have had a bad experience in the past. They might confide in you more once they get to know you a little better. Maybe you're the fourth realtor that they've met and they're tired of repeating themselves. Whatever. The key is to listen carefully to what buyers tell you, and to also carry the attitude that they may not be telling you the entire truth.

I could have written a book entitled "Things aren't always the way they seem to be," because it's come up so often in my selling career. Anyway, the flip side of this secret, skeptical attitude is an entirely different attitude. This is an attitude that most successful buyer's agents have already discovered. Maybe you have too. It goes something like this: **"My success is guaranteed one hundred per cent. I work hard and deserve success. I am going to win."**

You may not believe everything your clients tell you, but

you are absolutely convinced that you will succeed.

Hey, if **you** don't believe it, who will?

I remember after taking my first listing, the seller called me and said he wanted me to have an open house. It was my second month in real estate.

The night before my open house, I tossed and turned in bed. I worried that I was going to have too many people. I feared that I wouldn't be able to take care of all of them.

The day of my open house, it started to rain but that didn't discourage me. I drove around hammering yard stakes into the ground. Soon there were directional arrows for a three-block radius all pointing toward my open house. Then I hustled back inside the house as fast as I could. I figured that there was going to be a herd of buyers charging through the door at any minute, and I didn't want to miss anybody.

I knew that I was going to sell that house that day.

To my great surprise, not one person showed up.

I couldn't believe it. I even went outside and drove around the block to check to see that my signs were still up. (They were.)

Things aren't always the way they seem to be, right? But I didn't know that. I was so convinced that I would sell that home that day that I spent my time practicing, pretending what I'd say to a real buyer. I'd take out my pen and then I'd turn my pen to my imaginary client and say, "Mr. Buyer, I need your approval right here, please!"

Looking back now, I kind of feel sorry for the Callins. That was the name of the young couple who showed up at 4:00 that fateful afternoon. John and Rumi Callin. Who knows why they stopped in that day but I figured that they had to be serious buyers, looking at homes in the rain, so I didn't want to let them go. Every time they'd attempt to leave, I'd put my hand on the door and I'd show them something else about the house: how the ceiling didn't show any sign of leakage in any of the rooms. How nicely the fire burned in the fireplace. God it's almost embarrassing.

I was naïve enough to think that I was expected to sell the house to this couple on that afternoon, and that's exactly what I ended up doing.

The other agents in my office snickered when I came back. "Hey, Bob, how did your open house go?" they asked. "Get a lot of people in the rain?"

"I think I sold it," I answered truthfully.

"Right."

They couldn't believe it when I showed them the purchase agreement that I'd written. It was dumb luck, they claimed, and everyone wanted to touch my arm like I was made of gold or something. I ended up selling my first listing by myself. What's funny is that about three years later, Mr. and Mrs. Callin called me to list their home. They insisted that I hold open houses on it too because they knew that I would try hard to sell it myself. (I think they secretly wanted to see me torture another buyer, too.)

The point is that you need to realize that things aren't always going to be the way you think. But at the same time, you've got to have an ironclad, determined attitude that you will succeed and that you deserve success. You are worthy of success for all the hard work that you put in. All the crap that you take. All the unpleasant things you have to do. Sometimes you'll make sales just because of that ferocious determination. So here is my first piece of insider advice: take a deep breath and absorb these words: **"My success is guaranteed one hundred percent. I work hard and deserve success. I am going to win."**

Now exhale. Guess what?

Your success is now guaranteed! It feels good, doesn't it?

You may think I'm joking right now, but just imagine how you would feel if you knew that your success was guaranteed. You wouldn't care what people would say to you because you'd know you're going to win, right? You'd say to yourself, "Who cares what he or she thinks? I'm going to make this sale. I know I'm going to make it. I'm guaranteed."

Looking back at my real estate career, I thought that some of my sales seemed like downright flukes until I realized that I had instigated many of them. I was the one who helped make the decision for the buyers to buy. Just like the sale with the Callins, I'd expected people to buy from me and they did.

This is a discovery that I think most successful buyer's agents make.

Some of us think that we have to wait for buyers to tell us that they want to buy before we can start writing up a purchase agreement. It's like we expect to hear:

"Bob, we're ready to buy now."

"Okay, Mrs. Buyer. I'll alert the press."

But things aren't always the way they seem to be, right? If you expect that your clients should wait, guess what happens? They wait. If you expect them to put pen to paper, many times your clients will do it. They'll allow you to guide them, if you do it nicely.

Jack Nicklaus, the Hall of Fame golfer, was once asked by a sportswriter about how he'd made some of the tremendous putts in his career. Mr. Nicklaus thought for a minute and said, "I never missed a putt in my mind."

I think the secret to selling more homes to buyers starts right there. **Whenever you meet a new client, you mentally expect that person to buy from you.**

You know that things aren't **always** going to work out your way. If things don't work out, you still stay positive. You figure there is some good in everything that happens, so you keep right on going. You know that buyers aren't always going to roll over for you just because you have a ballsy attitude and think you're always going to win. You have to do the things necessary to be successful and work hard. Things aren't always going to be easy. But the secret of making a sale starts with that cocky belief that you will make it. Even if you just hit a bump in the road an hour ago with another client.

What about you? Are you on the right track right now? Before you guarantee your success, you have to rid your mind of any thoughts or attitudes of defeatism. All regrets, hates, resentments, superstitions and fears must go. You can't say, "I think I'll try it" because that doesn't cut it. Just for today, my friend, your mantra has got to be: **I am going**

to win.

What's another secret to help you become a surprising better real estate agent? That's what this book is all about, so read on!

CHAPTER TWO
How to Close Buyers

I've been selling real estate for almost 20 years, and during that time, I've helped lots of new full-time and part-time agents. Now it's been my experience that most of them can answer the phone and handle ad calls, they can build rapport with their prospects, and they can even show houses without knowing the right words to say. But I think that many agents blow the sale when it comes time to close. Why? **Because most agents haven't learned a surprisingly simple tool that I call, a 1-2-3 presentation.**

That's why I want to talk about the closing process. This is where I feel most agents, especially new or part-time agents, need to improve. This is what gave me the most problems when I was a new agent.

I think that for most buyer's agents one of the hardest things to do is to bridge the gap between the time when somebody **seems** to like a home to actually writing up the purchase contract. Here's what used to happen to me:

Bob: "Did you like the house?"

Client: "It was okay."

Bob: "You want to write it up?"

Client: "No. Let's see some more houses."

Bob: "Okay."

Sound familiar? Then two weeks later, as Yogi Berra says, "It's like deja vu all over again." I'd find myself saying, "Did you like the house?"

Client: "It was alright."

Bob: "You want to write it up?"

Client: "No. Let's see some more houses."

This kind of thing used to tear me up inside. I couldn't figure out how to bridge that gap. And I'd heard Tom Hopkins say that questions are the key and though I asked a lot of closing questions, I still couldn't bridge the gap. Then one day I was selling a home to some people who only spoke Spanish. And they asked me, in Spanish, this question: **What is the system of buying a home?** Now I had practiced telling sellers the system of selling a home (a listing presentation), but I'd never really practiced explaining to a buyer "how to buy."

Whenever I took a listing, for example, I was taught a script which began with the following lines. First I had to say to the seller, "How **long** have you lived here?" Then I'd say, "I bet you've really **liked** it, haven't you?"

And to help me memorize the entire presentation my sales trainer suggested I use various mnemonic devices. For example, I was supposed to stretch out my arms as wide as possible to remember "How long have you lived here?" Then I was supposed to pretend to lick an ice cream cone in order to remember, "I bet you've really liked (lick) it here, haven't you?"

In this way, step by step, I could memorize the entire listing presentation.

I say this because whether you realize it or not, when you close most buyers, you'll often do it the same way every time. In addition, very often you'll tell the buyer in advance what is going to be happening in the future.

One day, for example, I was showing homes to some pur-chasers who were wishy-washy. I'd showed them home after home but they couldn't seem to make up their minds about which home they liked the best. Finally I stopped the car in the middle of a parking lot and I said in a real smooth tone: "You know John, I kinda got a vibe that you really liked that last house."

John looked at me and said, "Are you crazy? I hated that house. In fact, right now I feel so frustrated that I'm ready to scream. Is this how most people buy houses? Tell me, Bob, and be honest. How do most people buy homes?"

And I was thinking on my feet as I answered because I still hadn't put everything together yet. I answered: "Well, John, it usually takes three steps. First we find the neighborhood, sec-ond we find the house, and third we fill out the paperwork. So let's start out with step number one. Which neighborhood felt most comfortable to you?"

John said: "I liked the first neighborhood you showed us the best." So we went back, found another home in that same neighborhood, and they bought it.

I figured that if one buyer had this question in mind, other buyers might too. So now whenever I meet with buyers, I figure that they might want to know how most people buy homes. So I tell them how the process works, just like I did with John. And I found that when buyers understood the process, I began to sell houses more easily!

How do most
people find homes?

Now I'm not advocating that you need to make a formal presentation with a flip chart, have a pre-purchasing book for buyers or a special kit, or give a slide presentation. Usually just a lined, yellow pad will work. The key is to realize that at a certain point it's helpful to stop asking questions and to outline to your clients what will be happening in the near future. Why do this? **Because the definition of closing a sale is helping a prospect rationalize making a buying decision.** Most buyers will allow you to help them to make a buying decision if:

- They like you.
- They think you know what you're doing.
- They know what to expect in the near future.

One of the ways I let buyers know in advance about what is going to be happening in the future is to give them what I call a **1-2-3 Presentation.**

What is a 1-2-3 Presentation?

A 1-2-3 Presentation is an explanation that briefly outlines, step by step, a buying or selling process. In

addition, it usually contains a summary statement about this process. I like to think of this statement as "what this means to you."

When I first meet with a buyer, for example, I want to let them know what to expect from me in the future so I'll start out with a 1-2-3 Presentation that goes something like this:

"Randy and Paula, before I show you any homes, I want to share with you how most people buy a home. It's so easy it can be broken down into three steps. **Step One:** We help you get pre-approved for your loan. **Step Two:** We help you find the right neighborhood. **Step Three:** We help you find the right home. What this means to you Randy, is that as your agent I'll be working very hard to find you the perfect home. So, tell me Paula, what kind of neighborhood and home do you and Randy have in mind?"

Now I shut up and listen.

Important: This technique is used to **supplement** asking questions. It's like the Chinese belief of yin and yang. If you talk too much, you lose people, right? **So you have to ask questions.** But if you ask too many questions, there might come a point where people might doubt whether you know what you're doing. A 1-2-3 Presentation helps you take charge or regain control.

Let's use this technique in a normal closing situation.

Example of a 1-2-3 Presentation for a First-Time Buyer

The purchasers, John and Mary, seem interested in a home. I pull into a fast-food restaurant, and when sitting before them, give the following presentation:

Bob: "John and Mary, many people think that buying a home is difficult, but it really isn't. In fact, there are just **six** easy steps. Whether you buy a home from me or somebody else, these steps are going to be the same. Here are the six steps to purchasing a home:

Step one: We fill out a purchase agreement form, like this **one.**

Step two: I'll bring the completed paperwork to **two** people: the seller and his agent. You don't come along with me.

It will be just me and them.

Step three: One of **three** things will happen: the seller will either accept, reject or counter your offer. If he accepts your offer, you move to the next step.

Step four: I'll open escrow and deposit your earnest money check in escrow. The escrow company will use this money **for** either your down payment or closing costs.

Step five: There are **five** things that your lender will need in order to make the loan for you. Some of these things we already have. They'll need:

1) credit report

2) appraisal

3) verification of employment

4) verification of deposit

5) termite report

Step six: Your loan is approved, and you'll pick up the keys from me the day that the deed records. Usually I'll have your keys by **six o'clock** at my office the day of closing. **What this means to you** is that I'll be there to guide you through the entire transaction. By the way John, were you thinking about offering full price on the home or slightly less?"

Now, by giving a 1-2-3 Presentation, I am telling the clients in advance, step by step, what to expect in the future. I seem to know what I'm doing, don't I? And buyers like to deal with people who know what they're doing, don't you agree? Do you notice how we can move right back into asking closing-type questions? Do you think that you could use this technique?

Full price or slightly less?

See? You're becoming a **surprisingly** better agent already!

Bob's Insider Advice: A 1-2-3 Presentation is a tool that should be used with special care. Practice your performance in advance and you'll appear more professional. Remember: the trick to being a bore is to tell everything you know about a subject. So keep it snappy!

CHAPTER THREE
Using the 1-2-3 Presentation

When else would you use a 1-2-3 Presentation? It can also be used whenever a real estate agent feels the need to take charge or reestablish control with a client. Giving a brief presentation allows the agent to take center stage.

It's like attending a seminar where all eyes are focused on the expert speaker who says, "I want to talk to you about the seven mistakes that most people make." Step by step, the speaker discusses the topic.

Can you repeat
step number 3 again?

Now, when an expert gives a speech, will the audience ignore the speaker or will they listen with rapt attention and take notes? If the speaker is good, or prepared, they'll listen. Sometimes there will even be somebody sitting in the back of the room who will say, "Can you repeat step number three again?"

When you give a 1-2-3 Presentation, for a brief period of time you stop asking closing questions and take the role of that expert speaker. Your audience is made up of your buyers and sellers. Because you can give 1-2-3 presentations to **sellers** as well as buyers.

A 1-2-3 Presentation for Listing Agents

Let's pretend that I have managed to list Mr. and Mrs. Seller's home and I am now their exclusive listing agent. One day, Betty, a buyer's agent with ABC Realty, calls me. She says she has an offer on my listing and wants to present it tonight to Mr. and Mrs. Seller.

What happens next?

That evening I go to the Seller's home and I introduce Betty to them. Then everybody moves into the kitchen where we gather around the table. Betty will give me one of her business cards, and I'll hand her one of mine.

Then before she presents her offer, I'll deliver a 1-2-3 Presentation that might go something like this:

"Mr. and Mrs. Seller, before Betty begins, I'd like to huddle up. In the next few minutes, three things are going to take place."

"First: Betty is going to tell us all about her clients and the contract that they've written."

"Second: Betty is going to leave the room so that we can discuss the details in private. At that time, I'll make up an estimated net sheet for you. That way you'll be able to see exactly how much money you'll be putting in your wallet after all the costs are taken out."

"Third: Betty will come back into the room and you'll either accept, reject or counter Betty's offer. **What this means to you** is that you'll know tonight if you'll be packing, right? Go ahead Betty, tell us about your buyers."

And then step by step the transaction continues.

If you're new in real estate, a step by step presentation like the one I gave to Mr. and Mrs. Seller can make you appear to know what you're doing. The Sellers are not going to say, "Why is Betty is leaving the room?" You seem to be in control of the situation. When people feel that somebody knows what they're doing, people tend to trust that person. Don't you agree?

Bob's Insider Advice: You probably have some good dialogues that you use with buyers and sellers. To become a surprisingly better agent, write out one of them as a step-by-step presentation, then stand up and practice giving it.

For example, you could talk about the six-step approach for buying a Freddie Mac property, or the five-step approach for buying a HUD home.

Question: Why should you stand up when you practice this presentation?

Answer: Because sometimes, when you're in a one-on-one selling situation with a buyer, every once in a while, just like when you make a listing presentation, **you'll suddenly stand up.** That's right, every once in a while you **stand up.**

This might sound crazy but every once in a while you might run into a "crunch-time" situation where drastic measures are needed.

I learned this technique by accident. There used to be a guy in my town named Jim Droz. He worked for Century 21 and he was a listing and selling machine. One year Jim Droz sold over 365 homes. Imagine going into a listing presentation and hearing the seller tell you, "By the way Bob, Jim Droz is coming over at seven o'clock, right after you."

Oh no, not Jim Droz, I would think. The name alone still sends a shiver down my spine.

This happened to me on eight different listing presentations, and I was zero for eight. The ninth time I heard it, I went into a panic. For some unknown reason, I stood up and began to give my listing presentation. I banged the table with my fist and waved my arms around. And when I was finished, the seller said, "Wow, I've never seen anybody get so excited about selling a condo for $48,000 in my entire life!" And he gave me the listing. I got two more listings after that.

I figured, "Hey, this standing up thing works!"

So every once in a while, I use it on my buyers.

Imagine this: John and Mary have just seen a home that they like and they're sitting across the table from me at Burger King. I'm thinking that they've got to write something up on this home because it's a seller's market and it's not going to last very long. Mary has another idea. She's saying something about seeing other houses. Suddenly, I rise to my feet and push my chair away:

Let me show you
how easy it is
to buy a home.

"John and Mary," I say, "there are three things you've got to keep in mind. One: houses in this area are only on the market for an average of fifteen days. That's the **average.** Two: right now we're in what's called a seller's market which means the competition for available homes gets tougher as time goes on. Three: right now it is very easy it is to become a homeowner, because the interest rates are low. **What this means to you,** is if you want to live in that home, in that neighborhood that you said you liked, the time to act is right now."

Question: Would standing up like that get Mary's attention? Sure. She'll probably say, "Sit down Bob, there are people here trying to eat." Or "Give me that paperwork so I can cover my face. Everybody's staring at us!"

Desperate times require desperate measures. So maybe you don't like standing up and giving a presentation at Burger King. Maybe you would feel more comfortable standing up in your conference room or office to give a presentation like that. No problem. Just remember, that to become surprisingly better at selling homes, whether you list homes or sell them, every once in a while, you might want to consider doing it **standing up**.

Why? By standing up and giving a presentation, even if it's to only one person, you make that buyer feel important and the matter seems more urgent. (Just make sure that you've practiced your performance and you know what you're going to say.)

Other Uses for 1-2-3 Presentations

A 1-2-3 Presentation can also be used for making some hard-to-explain real estate concepts easier to digest. By giving a buyer such an explanation, it makes a difficult subject easier to comprehend.

(Note: you don't have to stand up to give these presentations!)

Example: A Definition of Escrow

John, a first-home homebuyer, asks me, **"What exactly is escrow?"**

I could answer, "An escrow is an agreement between two or more parties providing that certain instruments be placed in a 3rd party for safekeeping."

Or I could give a 1-2-3 Presentation answer that might go something like this: "John, let me give you an example of an escrow. And I'm going to give it to you in three simple steps."

One: I want you to pretend that you're buying my pen for $10,000 cash.

You have the cash and I have the pink slip or deed for the pen.

Two: There are two questions to ask. Do you hand me the money first and hope that I give you the pink slip? Or do I hand you the pink slip and hope that you'll give me the cash?

Three: We both don't know one another very well so here's what we do.

We hire an independent third party, like Mary in the pink sweater, over there. She will act like the escrow company. I'll give my pink slip to Mary, and you'll also bring your cash to her. Then, when all the conditions of the purchase agreement have been fulfilled, Mary will give you the pink slip, or deed, and give me the money. **What this means to you** is that Mary makes sure that all of the seller's back taxes to the IRS are paid up, along with all of the homeowner dues, so you don't have to worry about paying any of the seller's bills when you buy the property. Mary makes sure that all the paperwork is done properly. Does that make sense to you? Do you see the importance of having an escrow?

I highlighted the "what this means to you" portion to restate a point. The key to a successful 1-2-3 Presentation is including a summary statement that tells the client what it means to them personally. Why is this information important to know? What effect will it have on their life? When you use the phrase **"what this means to you"** most people will perk up and really pay attention. Try it and see!

Reflections on the 1-2-3 Presentation

Now, it may seem tiresome to say "one, two, three or first, second, third" but I'm doing it deliberately to help you organize your thoughts. You might be the type of agent who likes to use *initials* instead of numbers. That's okay too. For example, you might tell a buyer about the three S's of a home inspection: **s**afety, **s**anitation and **s**ecurity. Just remember to also talk about "what this means to you".

I'm talking now to you, the reader. Would you agree with me that the 1-2-3 Presentation helps give the buyer some direction? Sure. The buyers aren't going to feel like idiots, for example, when you use the word escrow. You've taken the time to explain it to them without making them feel stupid.

Further Thoughts on Closing

I found that when I developed a 1-2-3 Presentation for buyers and used it to supplement the technique of asking closing questions I became more effective with buyers.

Another benefit to using a 1-2-3 Presentation is that it separates you from the rest of the pack. See, most agents are fond of telling clients *how difficult* it is to do something.

Thanks!

"Buying or selling a home is not easy," they'll say. Or "The state real estate exam is extremely difficult. It took me *ten times* to pass it." Now if this sounds like you, please stop making these kinds of announcements. Why?

Because when you give buyers a 1-2-3 Presentation, you're conveying the impression *that buying a home is easy,* and it can be done without much pain. Let me ask you a question: if you were a busy consumer, and who isn't these days, which real estate person would you rather work with? The real estate agent who makes everything seem difficult, and hard to accomplish, or the one who makes it simple and easy? After all, everybody's carrying a heavy load these days, aren't they? So let's make the burden a little lighter.

Buying or selling a home is simple and easy, isn't it? Sure.

In the next couple of chapters, I'm going to review a few more selling techniques one-on-one with you to help you close more buyers. But before I do, I'm going to go back and cover an inside secret of making sales stick. What secret do I have in mind?

Turn the page and find out!

CHAPTER FOUR
Prequalifying Purchasers

I'm going to back up now and talk about prequalifying buyers. You may already work with buyers who are preapproved or with purchasers who are willing to bring income documentation to your office or your lender's office. Even so, you may pick up some new ideas here. For those of you who don't yet take this step, this chapter will show you how you can easily deal with this issue.

I'll start by giving you an example of how I communicate with a new client who calls in response to one of my ads. There are three or four questions that I ask a prospect on the telephone. I want to know:

a) How's your credit?

b) Have you been prequalified with a lender. And if so, which one?

c) Are you currently working with another agent?

d) How is your schedule for getting together tonight, or Saturday?

Example: Responding to the Initial Call

"Good morning, Bob Boog Realty, how may I help you?"

"I'm calling on the Sexy Townhouse ad I saw advertised in the *LA Times*."

"No problem sir, let me check to see if it's still available. May I place you on hold for just a few seconds?"

"Go."

(After coming back) "That is a lovely home. It features

newer carpet, fresh paint and a spacious kitchen. By the way, my name is Bob, and your name is..."

"My name is Andre."

"Hi Andre, can I get your telephone number?

"Not just yet. I don't want people bothering me."

"No problem. Are you looking to buy anytime soon?"

"I don't know yet. I'm just getting started."

"Fair enough. Have you gotten prequalified with a lender yet?"

"No, not yet."

"The reason I ask is that many sellers want to see a preapproval letter from a lender when we submit an offer. It's a good thing to do, because then you know more intelligently what price range to look in. I mean I'd hate to have you fall in love with the perfect home and then get beaten by another purchaser who had the foresight to obtain a preapproval letter in advance. By the way, Andre, how is your credit?"

"Pretty good, I think."

"Great. What I'd like to do is fax you a credit authorization form and have you fax it back to me so that my lender can run a quickie credit check. It's free and if nothing else you'll get to see what your credit report looks like. Sometimes we have problems with somebody else's bad credit showing up on a client's credit report. If that happens to you, it's best to take care of it right away. Would it be okay with you if I fax a credit authorization form over to you now?"

"I guess so."

"What's your fax number?"

"555-5555."

"Great. I'm going to fax this right over to you. I'd like to get together with you on Saturday if that's okay. I'll need you to bring me these **three** items. Ready? I want you to bring me …**One:** Enough paystubs for one month, **Two:** The last **two** years' tax returns, and **Three:** Three bank statements."

"If you can't find your bank statements bring me what you've got. OK? Also I'll need to get your home telephone number."

Now the client and I are off to a good start!

Note: Here is what you'll tell most clients to bring

One: Paystubs for 1 month (last month).
Two: Last 2 years W-2's or tax returns.
Three: Last 3 bank statements.

Why I Want the Buyer to Bring Their Income Documentation to My Office

There are three good reasons why I use this approach with buyers.

One: It separates the lookers from the buyers. Lookers will hang up the phone or not come into the office with their stuff. Serious buyers show up with the requested information.

Two: It gives me a sense of control. Andre probably isn't going to be looking with any other real estate agent this weekend. Why? He's trusting me with his paperwork.

Three: It helps cement a loyal, lucky relationship with me as his buyer's agent. When Andre comes to my office, I'm also going to have him sign a client registration agreement and an agency disclosure. After he's signed a couple of documents and has given me his income tax info and paystubs, a feeling of loyalty is generated. Do you follow me? *He's trusting me.*

Question: Suppose my buyers can't find their tax returns? What then?

Answer: If the tax forms were filled in by a paid preparer, check to see if you can get a copy from the preparer. This way may save time and money. Otherwise, have your clients write or visit an IRS office. (The toll-free telephone number for the nearest office is listed in your telephone directory). Tell them to obtain a copy of form 4506, "Request for Copy of Transcript of Tax Form". It costs about $14.00 for a copy of each tax period and they need to send full payment with their request. Tell them to expect to receive their copies in about ten working days after the IRS receives their request.

I keep a stack of credit authorization forms in my brief-case so that if I meet new purchasers at an open house, they can fill it out, sign it, and I can fax it to my lender. That way I can gauge how motivated they are.

Note: If your client is self-employed you'll need:

One: One profit & loss statement.
Two: Last two years' tax returns.
Three: Last three bank statements.
Four: Last twelve months of bank statements.

CREDIT AUTHORIZATION FORM

I, we)___Juan & Maria Lopez_____ authorize
_____Bill Jones_____of_____Acme_____Mortgage Co.
to obtain a copy of my credit report.

Please advise <u>Bob Boog</u>, my real estate agent of my credit.

My information is as follows: Date: ___01/09/99_____

Last name: ___Lopez___ First Name: ___Juan_____

Street Address: _115 Main St._   City: <u>Yourtown</u> State: <u>MN</u>

Zip Code:<u>12345</u> Date of Birth:_____08/10/62_____

Home phone:___222-333-4444___ Work Phone: _222 555-3333_

Social Security Account Number: ___111-11-1111_____

Co-borrower Last Name:___Lopez___First Name:_Maria___

Street Address: _115 Main St._   City: <u>Yourtown</u> State: <u>MN</u>

Zip Code:<u>12345</u> Date of Birth:_____01/04/62_____

Co-borrower SS#__333-44-5555_ Work Phone: _222- 555-3330_

Borrower Signature: _____*Juan Lopez*_____

Co-borrower Signature: ____*Maria Lopez*_____

Question: Why is buyer motivation important?

Answer: Because it's the key to spending time with a purchaser. Many new agents ask me, "How do you know which buyers to work with and which ones to let go?" The simple answer is to work only with the motivated buyers and let the unmotivated ones go.

But the truth is things aren't always the way they seem to be. New agents often give up on good buyers because they think that a finicky buyer is not motivated when all they really are is just undecided. Most buyers fall into one of four motivation categories: They are: 1.) Ready and Willing, 2.) Special-home Motivated, 3.) Steal of a Deal, or 4.) Casual Shopper.

1. People who are in the Ready and Willing Category are ready, willing and able to purchase in the next 30 days. He or she promptly brings you all of his income documentation, has good credit, and **will meet you Friday night at ten o'clock in a dark alley of a bad neighborhood in order to see a home!** These people are not only ready and willing, they are itching to buy!

2. People who are in the Special-home category want to purchase a home that suits their own special needs. For example: the home *must* have 3,000 sq. ft., hardwood floors and a pool. This buyer sometimes becomes motivated if they see something that they really like, but oftentimes they still will hesitate. Why? *Because special-home buyers are often afraid of making a bad decision.* Sometimes you have to tell them that because they may never find the perfect home. So find out what's **most** important to them. **"Monica, is the reason that you're hesitating because you're afraid of making a bad decision? (yes) What's the key issue to you? Is it the pool? Is it the floors?"** The special-home buyer needs plenty of information, understanding and patience. Pin them down with questions to better assist them.

3. People who belong to the Steal-of-a-Deal category will purchase today if the price is low enough, but usually it's not. Don't expect him or her to be loyal to you. They often spread the news to ten real estate agents that they're in the market for a home, so get something in writing if you decide to work with them.

4. The people in the Casual Shopper category are the least motivated and are usually just looking. Sometimes he or she wants you to drive them all around town. Why? *Because they feel it's your job.* They'll tell you whatever you want to hear in order to get you to do it too. They'll say, "Gee Bob, we misplaced our prequalification letter. But don't worry, we've got lots of money. Let's just see some homes!" (Really they don't have a pot to pee in.) Or they haven't done their taxes yet. They'll say, "I left my tax information at my accountant's office and he or she is on vacation." Whatever. This buyer sometimes wants you to spend lots of time with them without giving you a commitment. Why? *They think it's your job.*

Question: How do you tell the difference between the Casual Shopper and the Special-home buyer?

Answer: The Special-home buyer will give you his or her income documentation. The Casual Shopper doesn't.

That's why I recommend that you get factual information on people before they step into your car. Face it: *It's not your job to drive casual buyers around town.* Let them drive themselves. There are too many good buyers out there. Fax casual buyers a list of homes and a map and let them drive themselves around. Microsoft has a nice CD-ROM program that makes up maps. You can print out a map and insert the prices of homes in the little bubbles that point to the street or get a map from **www.maps.yahoo.com.** If these buyers are really sincere about buying they'll get prequalified.

I'm serious. This is the killer mistake that sends most people running right out the real estate business. They think to themselves, "Hey, these buyers appear to have lots of money. All I need to do is find them one home, and then I'll get their income information." Then after showing home after home to buyers who never buy, the agent finally gives up.

Bob's Insider Advice: People who are not motivated to buy rarely jump through the hoops of getting preapproved for a loan. They often have nothing better to do on a Sunday than to waste your time. Don't let them!

Please note: many ready and willing buyers start out as casual shoppers. They first make a fact-finding mission to an area to see if they can afford it. For this reason, please be courteous. Make up a folder filled with facts about your local community. You can download information on the Internet or get this information free at the local chamber of commerce. Staple your business card to the folder, give them a map, and who knows? They may remember you and come back to buy a home from you!

The Awful Truth

An agent in my office was working with a buyer who was a police officer. He'd been referred from a friend and he said that his combined income was over $80,000 a year. Now he wouldn't sign a credit authorization or provide income documentation because he claimed he'd been preapproved for a loan by a mortgage broker. This cop was very tight-lipped. He said that he was concerned about his privacy. His story sounded believable, didn't it? Police officers are often concerned about their privacy and many have friends who are mortgage brokers. So what happened? After showing homes for two days with no results, she told him **the awful truth** which goes something like this:

"Mr. and Mrs. Johnson, I've enjoyed meeting you and showing you homes but, I can't continue working like this. I work on a commission-only basis and if I don't make a sale, I can't pay my bills. For us to continue working together, I'll need you to sign a form that states that you're willing to buy exclusively from me within the next three months. If not, then I'm sorry, but you're going to have to find another agent." (Now, some agents ask for a $600 deposit at this point.)

Guess what the policeman said? "Sign something with you? Oh, in that case, I won't waste your time. I'm really not planning to buy for at least six months. I'll call you when I'm ready."

That agent could have shown homes every day for a week and not sold him anything, right? Why? *Because the buyer wasn't motivated.* Either that or the buyer didn't like her. And if that's the case, he's still not going to buy from her anyway, is he? No. Better to find out sooner than later, don't you agree?

To find out how motivated a buyer is, start by asking questions when you're at the office or while on the phone. Questions like: "Why are you moving?" "When does your lease expire?" "Do you live around here?" "Do you have any friends who live around here?" "Have you seen any homes so far that you've liked?" "Have you been working with any other agents?" Now, every so often you'll run into a Cranky Carl. Cranky Carl has purchased 13 homes in the past ten years and he thinks that he knows more than **anybody** about real estate. Old Carl doesn't want to be bothered with providing income documentation. He's purchased thirteen homes before and nobody else has ever asked him to sign a credit authorization form. One way to handle him is to say:

"I understand how you feel Carl, and many of our clients have felt the same way. What we've found however, is that nowadays many credit reports have erroneous information on them. Rather than waiting to take care of a problem down the road, why don't we make sure that it's okay right now? Does that make sense to you, Carl?"

A Note to Those Using a Different Approach

You might be saying to yourself: Bob, I work differently from you. My company says that I should use the Internet which allows me to access a credit reporting agency through my palmtop and I then use a *"Top Qualifier"* software package and blah, blah, blah. Or Bob, I can't do what you advise. I have special office addendums and then my mentor agent goes over the purchase contract with me.

If you typically do things differently, wonderful. But for those of you who don't ask for income documentation from buyers, try it my way once and see what happens.

Still Have Questions?

At this point, let's look at some questions that commonly come up for agents regarding prequalifying buyers.

Question: I have a purchaser with a 20% down payment. Does the buyer still need to bring me their tax returns?

Answer: Good question. The answer depends on your lender. In my area, a lender can finance most buyers on an "easy qualifyer" loan with 20% down. Your area may be different. I would want to see a bank statement that shows that the client does have the money in the bank or truly does have access to the funds.

Question: "Bob, I do things differently. I always have my buyers call my lender directly and then after the buyer has met with the lender, I show property. Isn't this a better way to work than having the buyers bring their income documentation to me?"

Answer: Not in my opinion, but if it works for you, fine. I like an agent to be in control. If the lender has all the income documentation then he is in control. He'll still make the loan if you don't make the sale, right? What happens if your lender takes a three week vacation? Or if he or she "accidentally" tells another buyer's agent about your buyer? Who loses? You do. It's much easier to change lenders if you still have the buyer's income documentation, right? You can just fax it to lender number two.

Summing It All Up

Don't take the lazy way out; that's the surprising secret to prequalifying purchasers properly. If you have a prequalification program on your computer, use it to get an **approximate** amount. But you'll become more effective if you get the purchaser's actual documentation. Things aren't always the way they seem to be, remember? Too many times buyers tell you that they work forty hours a week but they really only work thirty-two. Or they tell you they made $95,000 last year and they really only paid taxes on $44,000. Or they say they have perfect credit and their credit shows seven 90-day lates and a car that's been repossessed. Get your clients to sign a credit authorization, copy their documentation, and play your cards close to your vest. If the credit looks good, great, then move forward.

CHAPTER FIVE
The Bridge Before the Close

We talked in the last chapter about opening the sale which involves prequalifying the buyer and showing property. Now Chapters 8 through 12 discuss showing property, so in this chapter I still want to talk about closing the sale. In particular, a surprisingly simple component that I call, **The Bridge Before the Close.**

First, what do I mean by bridge? A bridge is a memorized speech that sounds nonchalant but gets you into position to close the sale. In my case, when I was new in real estate, I would be driving the car knowing that my clients loved a particular home and wanted to buy it, but I didn't know how to easily get them out of my car to signing the contract. **A bridge moves you and your clients from one place to another without the client fighting you.**

Here's an example. Tom and Melinda are preapproved to purchase a home up to $150,000 and I've shown them three properties, and they both love one of them. But now Melinda says, "I'd still like to see more homes."

What do I do? First, I give them what they want. If Melinda wants to see another home, no problem, I'll show her another home.

Then after viewing that home, I'll check her pulse.

Bob: "So Melinda, how did you feel about that home?" Or:

Bob: "I kinda got a feeling that you still like that first home."

Note: whenever you hear Tom or Melinda say, "That home was nice but I still really love that first home," drive to a place where you can sit down face to face with them. Without asking, for example, I'll nonchalantly park the car near a coffee shop, a fast-food restaurant or a city park. Then I'll use a bridge:

"Tom and Melinda, let's take a break for just a few minutes. I need to use the washroom. Then **I'd like to go over**

51

some items that may be of interest to you. After that, we can figure out where you want to go next, okay?"

What are they going to say? No, you can't use the bathroom?

Another good bridge is:

"I'd like to give you some numbers so you'll have something to think about tonight."

Or: "I'd like to show you what has sold in the area to give you an idea what is happening in the neighborhood."

All of the above are examples of what I call a bridge.

A bridge then, is a nonchalant offer or statement that is used to position a salesperson for the close. After all, why did you drive them around with you all morning? To sell them a house, right? What I mean by this is that sometimes agents drive around all day with one couple and never put themselves in a position to close. They'll go to a restaurant alright, but they'll leave the purchase agreement, briefcase, calculator and pen in their car. Or they'll come back to the office with the client and allow them to leave empty-handed.

But when you tell a client, "Jason, I'd like to give you some numbers to think about tonight," what does it allow you to do? It gives you the opportunity to open your briefcase, take out a calculator, a yellow legal tablet and a purchase agreement. And you do this very nonchalantly. You're a professional who does this kind of thing all the time.

People who are serious about purchasing a home won't even notice that you're shaking like a Cuban space shuttle.

Now sometimes I'll use a bridge simply to check a client's motivation pulse. If I suspect that Tom and Melinda have champagne tastes, I might say:

"Tom I want to sit down and go over some items with you." Now Melinda's eyes might pop out of her head when she watches me place a purchase agreement on the table. Right? She might answer, "That's okay, Bob, we're not in any hurry. We can live at our mom's house without paying rent for another year." What does that tell me? I know that Tom and Melinda are not very motivated, right? If this happens, why not politely tell your clients: "No problem, feel free to take your time. In fact, I have an idea. Here is a scratch pad and a list of homes in your price range. Jot down the addresses that look interesting to you. Then when I have a little more time, we can get together again and look at the insides of these homes."

On the other hand, if Tom has been transferred from out of town and only has two days to make a decision, you're going to wear pajamas under your work clothes, right? Tom and Melinda are either going to buy from you or die!

Again, when I sit face to face with them, I'll have these items with me: a calculator, two pens and a yellow legal pad. And normally, if I feel they're ready, I will have a blank purchase contract inside my legal pad.

Zig Ziglar calls a legal pad a salesman's "talking book" and I agree. I think a lined, yellow pad is invaluable to a buyer's agent. Why? It can be used as a visual aid, and it helps do the talking for you.

I'm Wearing My Pajamas Underneath!

So let's listen as I sit across from Tom and Melinda at the table.

"Tom and Melinda, I know exactly how you feel. You're probably a little nervous right now, right? Believe me, many people have felt the same way as you. What we've found, however, is that understanding how the process works makes things a lot easier."

Now at this time, I might talk about how easy it is to purchase a home. But if Tom and Melinda are familiar with the process, I'll probably use one of these two presentations. They are **The Paperwork Presentation** or **The Full Price or Slightly Lower Presentation**. Here's how they work:

The Paperwork Presentation

This may seem to be rather bold, but you take out the purchase agreement from your legal pad and lay it on the table. Then you say: "Tom and Melinda, this is the paperwork that we use to present an offer to a seller. It's a standard California Association of Realtors purchase agreement, and I wanted to show it to you so you could see for yourself what it looks like. It's filled with protection for you and it's really easy to fill out. Paragraph X, for example, gives you the right to hire a home inspector to thoroughly investigate the property. Paragraph Y states that the roof shall be leak free. Oh and Paragraph Q allows us to ask the seller to pay for a one-year home warranty for you. What exactly is a home warranty? Let me explain it to you."

Can you
tell that I'm
a little nervous?

I think you get the picture. By explaining how things work, you reduce the fear and anxiety of making the purchase. You're making it easier for them to buy. You're opening the door and showing them that there is nobody in the dark room. And if they have any questions about the purchase contract, who is there to explain it to them? You are. You're the expert, letting them know how the process works. Now eventually you'll say:

"Let's see...this property is listed for $100,000, did you want me to write it up at full price or slightly lower?"

Please note: If a buyer is interested in writing up an offer on a house, without giving a presentation, shut up, stop crossing the bridge and start writing! Sometimes people will want you to start writing up the contract without any persuasion whatsoever.

The next presentation is a little more direct. This you might want to use on somebody who is a little more sophisticated. Have a calculator and a pen ready when you use it!

The "Full-Price or Slightly Lower" Presentation

Bob: "Brad and Nicole, I want to give you some **numbers** that you can take home and think about. First though, I need you to give me a **price** so that I can calculate the payments. Shall I compute based on the **list price** or **slightly lower**?" (What do you think 99% of people are going to say?)

Brad: "Slightly lower."

Bob: "It's listed at $100,000. What are you thinking?"

Brad: "Let's try it at $90,000."

Bob: "Mmm. I was thinking more like $95,000. Let me do the math on **both** for you. Your down payment at $95,000 is only $2,850. Your down payment with the same 3% down would be $2,700 at $90,000. That's not that much different, is it?"

(Note: This is a pretty common scenario. Many buyers when you say "slightly lower" don't know what to offer and will throw out a figure just to get the ball rolling. Realize that they are looking to you for guidance. If you feel market value really is $90,000, write it for $90,000. If $90,000 is too low, (or more than 10% lower than the purchase price) try to gently nudge the buyer up to what a seller might reasonably consider. (2% - 5% lower than the purchase price.)

Bob: "When would you like to take possession, 30 or 45 days?"

Brad: "Which is better?"

Now you can talk about the buyer's closing costs.

Bob: "I've got an idea. We could ask the seller to pay part of your closing costs. How about writing this for $96,200 and asking the seller to pay $1,200 towards your closing costs? By the way, Brad, this is the paperwork that we give to the sellers. All real estate agreements have to be in writing. Nicole, did you want the seller to leave those curtains that you liked in the kitchen?"

And now you're on your way to making a sale!

Bob's Insider Advice: Bridging a sale like this can also make you appear surprisingly "pushy" so you have to handle the buyer carefully. Practice role-playing this technique with a fellow agent first, before using it on a buyer. Also, it often helps to show purchasers what comparable properties have sold for, so it's nice to bring along some comparable sales information or have access to a computer. If at any time a buyer starts to resist, explain that by getting the numbers down in writing now, the buyer will have more details to think about later.

Also, if you are showing a HUD home or a VA repossession where the buyer enters a sealed bid auction and must make the highest offer possible to win, your strategy is going to be completely different. We'll talk more about raising the offering price in Chapter 6.

Romancing the Buyer

I guess what I'm saying is **be nice but don't be too pushy**. Some agents forget that we're not selling shirts. Buying a home is a big investment and people get turned off when you pressure them too much. Sometimes you have to romance a buyer before they'll make a commitment. Some agents call it rapport but I call it romancing because most buyers want you to spend time with them and call them on the phone. You'll give them compliments and send them thank you notes. You'll ask questions about their interests. When the buyers seem to really like the home or the neighborhood, you sit down and show them the numbers. Otherwise, if the time isn't right, just talk about the homes you've seen and set a date to get together again.

Attention: Brand New Full-time or Part-time Agents

If you are brand new to real estate and are afraid of closing a sale or making a mistake on a purchase agreement, I know exactly how you feel. I think it's sometimes better for you to tell your clients to go home and relax so you can fill out the purchase agreement in private. You might want to use a 1-2-3 Presentation that goes something like this: "Melody, I told you I was new and I don't want to make any mistakes, so I like to take a three-step approach.

Step one: You give me the price, full price or lower, that you want to pay and I'll write it down here on my yellow pad.

Step two: You can go home and take a breather.

Step three: I'll come over to your house tonight with all the paperwork filled out. After you sign everything, I'll bring the papers back to my broker to review. **What this means to you** is that I'll make sure that everything is done correctly before I bring it to the seller. Fair enough?"

Help! I'm new and I don't know what I'm doing!

This presentation is not too difficult is it? When you're new in real estate, sometimes it's hard to concentrate. The clients may have questions, their children may be running around, you feel nervous, under pressure, and it's easy to make mistakes. So give yourself some breathing room. Tell them "I need a little time to get everything done correctly for you," not "I need to find a contract I can copy from because I have no idea what I'm doing."

If you need to fill out a purchase agreement in the privacy of a sound-proof room, do it. Most clients will understand. Because when you tell them that you want to do the right thing and have your broker look over the paperwork, they'll appreciate your concern for them. Do it this way until you feel comfortable filling out purchase agreements on your own. (With your broker's approval, of course!)

Now somewhere along the line I realized that I was more comfortable selling homes when I practiced my communication. Many times when agents say that their buyers didn't like anything, it's not always because the clients are stupid. Sometimes the agent isn't showing the right homes, sometimes they bring buyers to the wrong neighborhood, and sometimes it's not either one. Sometimes it's what the agent is saying, or not saying.

In other words, one time I was in a sales slump and I picked out a home for some clients, but I asked another agent to show it to them. This agent worked part-time in real estate and it actually surprised me when the clients bought the home. Then it dawned on me that maybe it wasn't the homes I was showing. Maybe I wasn't doing a good enough job communicating.

But how could I improve?

Would you like to learn how to communicate better with your clients? Read on, my friends.

"Whenever I meet someone, I try to imagine
him wearing an invisible sign that says,
"Make me feel important." I respond to
this sign immediately, and it works wonders."
— Mary Kay Ash, *Mary Kay Cosmetics*

CHAPTER SIX
Feel, Felt, Found

In this chapter, I'm going to focus on a closing strategy called "Feel, Felt, Found."

The next chapter will review six other closing techniques, but Chapter Six will look at this single approach. Why spend so much time on it? Because it works!

Feel, Felt, Found is based on three phrases that are used in the same order each time. These are:

"I understand how you feel."

"Many people have felt the same way."

"What we've found, however, is…"

Now I'm not suggesting that I invented this technique. Feel, Felt, Found is as old as dirt and was taught to me by a colleague who worked in retail sales. However it hasn't been utilized much in real estate.

But in the last few years the real estate market has changed. In the past, buyers didn't bring their income documentation into the real estate office. They gave it to a mortgage banker who often waited for the buyer to find the perfect home and then the banker would try to arrange the financing. Nowadays, however, I don't want to waste my time showing homes until I know that my purchaser has been pre-qualified, which poses a different sort of problem.

Here's what I mean. When a buyer brings his or her income documentation to my office, signs a credit authorization form, and is told that he or she is qualified to buy up to a certain price, that buyer is ready to buy.

Wouldn't you agree? The money starts to burn a hole in their pocket! So usually I don't have a problem asking a buyer to write an offer. It's just that the buyer wants to write a low offer.

Sure. That buyer feels empowered. He or she feels like they're in the driver's seat. Not only that, but many of them will tell you about friends or relatives who got a steal of a deal. Here is typical story of one of these not-so-rare breed of client. See if it sounds familiar to you.

The Typical Low-Bidding Buyer Story

"The reason I want to offer so low, Bob, is because of what happened when my father bought his last home. See my father looked at a hundred homes. He hated most of the houses the realtor showed him, but he was only qualified up to $65,000. The homes he liked were all listed for over $100,000. Finally my father saw one home that he really liked and it was listed for $115,000. He offered $65,000 – and boy did his real estate agent get mad! She didn't even want to present it, but to her great surprise the seller accepted my father's offer. The seller let the property go for $45,000 less than his asking price."

Don't you just hate it when buyers tell you those kinds of stories? And usually they'll have this annoyingly smug look on their faces too.

Coping with the Challenge Using Feel, Felt, Found

How do we convince a buyer to come up in price? How is this accomplished? How do you communicate to a buyer that it's in his or her best interest to increase the price? Especially when working with somebody who has been staying up late at night watching infomercials and now wants to steal something? Or how do you nudge your HUD home buyers or VA Repo buyers to go up in price?

My advice is that you first try **"FEEL, FELT, FOUND."** Then if it doesn't work, use one of the other traditional closes found in the next chapter of this book. Let's review some closing strategies used with the low-bidding buyer utilizing the Feel, Felt, Found method.

Client #1: "We know this home is listed for $178,000, but we wanted to offer the seller $150,000."

"I understand how you **feel, Paul. You want to get a good value.**

"Many buyers have **felt** the same way."

"What we've found, however, is that when you buy a home you're also buying the neighborhood. Sometimes a quality neighborhood is hard to find. You do like the excellent schools and the safety this neighborhood provides, don't you?"

Let's examine how this technique works.

One: When you first say, "I understand how you feel," I think it's also important that you **immediately repeat or rephrase the buyer's objection.** In this way, you are acknowledging the buyer's concern. So if the buyer says, "The bedrooms are too small," what would you say? "Right. I understand how you feel. The bedrooms are too small."

Two: When you tell the buyer that many buyers have felt the same way, it validates that concern for them. They aren't going crazy. They are normal to feel such a way. They are like everybody else.

Three: That sets us up for the zinger. **"However what we've found is... blah, blah, blah."** When you say this, you'd better start firing some good ammo. This is your chance to shoot them down, so you'd better hit them with a powerful reason that they might not have considered.

Hit me with your best shot!

Client #2: "This HUD home is listed on the Internet for $57,000 so we thought a good offer for it might be $46,000."

"I understand how you **feel,** Virginia. You're looking to get a good value. Many purchasers that I've worked with in the past have **felt** the same as you. What we've **found** however is that most people who win sealed bid auctions make aggressive bids. By this I mean, they make a bid that win or lose they gave it their best shot. We had one client, for example, who lost a bid by $7,000 who couldn't sleep at night. Why? It was knowing that for just $48.00 more a month the property could have been hers. I'd hate to have you lose this great opportunity for just a few dollars a month. Let me show you how much your payments will be at $63,500. Your down payment will go up only slightly and you won't be throwing your money away on rent any more."

It's amazing how well Feel, Felt, Found works! Please don't change the order. Let's look at another way to use it.

Client #3: "Maybe we should wait till the interest rate goes down."

"I understand how you **feel,** Roxanne. If you're like most people, you probably feel a little nervous right now. Many purchasers that I've worked with have **felt** the same as you. What we've **found,** however, is that when the interest rate changes, prices usually go up too. Let me show you what homes in this neighborhood have sold for and you can see what a great value you're getting."

(Now show comparable sales from the multiple listing system.)

Client #4: "Looks good Bob, but my dad said to offer 20% less."

Bob: "Got it. I can understand how you **feel,** Michael, your father is interested in looking out for you and wants to make sure that you get a good deal. Believe me, many of my clients have **felt** the same way. What we've **found,** however, is that sometimes relatives tend to be a little negative. Do you know why? Because they don't want to be blamed if something goes wrong in the future. I mean then they can say, 'I told you so, Michael.' But they haven't been out driving around looking for places. Right? They don't know how difficult it is to find a nice home in a decent neighborhood."

Client #5: "This home is listed for $210,000, do you think the seller will take $190,000 for it?"

"Leon, my crystal ball is still at the shop getting fixed. But I know how you feel. You want to get a good value, right? And believe me, I respect that. In fact, many buyers have felt the same way. Is the reason you're offering $190,000 because you really only want to pay $200,000 for the home? (Yes.) What we've found, however, is that nowadays many sellers will simply reject a low offer rather than counter. In fact if you're serious about purchasing the home for $200,000, let's write the offer for slightly more than $200,000 and ask the seller to pay some of your closing costs. Why? Because it will sound better to the seller. Sometimes when an offer is too low, the seller takes it personally and won't even issue a counteroffer. I've got an idea. Why don't we try it at $203,000 and ask the seller to pay $3,000 of closing costs? That way the seller won't feel offended and your offer will be closer to what you want. Let me show you how it looks on paper."

Do you see how to read this buyer? I subtracted the buyer's offer of $190,000 from the asking price of $210,000. That leaves a difference of $20,000. $20,000/2 = $10,000. $190,000 + $10,000 = $200,000.

Now, there is no guarantee the seller will accept an offer of $203,000, is there? No. But let's face it. Aren't I a little bit closer to making a sale when I get the buyer to improve on his original offer? (Say yes.)

Bob's Insider Advice: Try to get your contracts written as close to full price as possible! You'll make more sales if you do!

Final Remarks on Feel, Felt, Found

Like all techniques, Feel, Felt, Found will not work with everybody. There will always be an exception. I mean some people are so tight that they squeak when they walk and they'll refuse to budge a penny, no matter what you tell them. Do you have clients like that? Too bad. You may need to find some new ones.

But Feel, Felt, Found works well on most people which is good because sometimes when you're trying to close a transaction a funny thing happens. Many buyers have had some kind of sales training in their background and they may actually recognize *other* closes. I once had a buyer say, "Oh I know that one, you're using the Ben Franklin close, right?"

But that usually doesn't happen with Feel, Felt, Found. What I like about it is that this close comes across sounding natural once you get the hang of it. It doesn't sound like a memorized script. Try it tomorrow and see!

Okay, we've got one closing technique down and there are more to go. Let's move on to the next chapter and work on improving your selling skills with six additional approaches. Are you feeling more confident now? (Say yes!) Good!

I feel like I found what I felt and I find that feels good.

How do you feel about that?

Help the other fellow recognize what he wants, then help him decide how to get it. Figure out what is the key issue?

— Frank Bettger

CHAPTER SEVEN
Six Traditional Closes

Let's set the stage: your client, Mark, is balking at signing a purchase agreement or suggests a price that seems unrealistically low.

Instead of jumping for joy and writing up a low offer, let's try our best to improve the offer, knowing that what we're doing is good for them. There is only a limited amount of homes at this time on the market, and Mark seems to like the neighborhood. This time we're going to use one of the six traditional real estate closes. The secret to utilizing these closes is to act natural. You know exactly what you're doing and your client doesn't know that you do. That gives you an advantage.

1) The Similar Situation Close:

In this close, the agent tells the buyer about another buyer who had a similar problem and how the agent successfully solved the problem. Example: "No problem, Mark, many people have felt the same way. Recently I worked with some folks from Chicago. These people really had it bad. Not only were they buying their first home but they were moving from a place where homes were a lot less expensive. So here's what we did. We went to the computer and I pulled up all the comparable homes in the neighborhood that had sold, and then we used this information to write up the paperwork that we gave to the seller. They are so happy in their new home that they even sent me a thank you card." Important: please don't lie about the comparable sales and don't be too boastful about the sales you've made.

2) The Ben Franklin or Balance Sheet Close:

In this close, the agent compares what the buyer likes best about the property and what they don't. **Phraseology: "Let's make a list of all the yeas of this home. Now let's write down the nays. It looks like the answer is pretty obvious, doesn't it?"**

Example: "Mark, I know how you feel. You're kind of nervous and you want to make sure that you get a good value, right? Don't worry, this is normal. Many purchasers have felt the same way. What we have found is that if you take a sheet of paper and list all the benefits of living in this home, as well as all the negatives, the answer pretty much jumps out at you. Let's do it, shall we? We'll put the Yeas on one side and the Nays on the other."

Yeas	Nays
1) Three car garage	1) Needs interior paint
2) Gigantic family room with fireplace	2) Small kitchen
3) Community bike paths	
4) Excellent pride of ownership	
5) Spacious back yard	
6) Has a new roof	

"Well, the answer looks pretty obvious to me. How do you feel about it, Mark? Shall we write it up then?"

Note: the *Counter Offer Comparison Sheet* found on page 185 is a stepchild of this traditional technique. Use it to explain counter-offers to buyers.

3) The "Okay I Need You to Sign Here Please" Close:

This is a direct close where the agent cuts to the chase and simply asks for the order. "Ok, Mark, I just need your approval right here, please."

Ok, I need you to sign here, please.

4) The "I Wanna Think it Over" Close:

"That's fine, Mark, I understand how you feel. I mean you wouldn't take your time thinking it over unless you were seriously interested, right? I mean you're not saying this just to get rid of me, are you? Good. So you're going to give this decision some very careful consideration. (Beat) By the way, Mark, just to clarify my thinking, what is it exactly that you need to think over? Is it the landscaping? Is it the neighborhood? Is it the price?"

"You're not saying this to get rid of me are you?"

5) The Purchase Agreement Close:

In this close, the agent asks questions necessary to fill out the purchase agreement and then writes the answers down in the purchase agreement. This is an assumptive close and should be used with caution as it will definitely make you appear to be pushy. However, it's a good close to use when you have a motivated client. "Do you use a middle initial, Mark? Great, let me write that down, Mark W. Smith. You did want to ask the seller to include the window treatments, didn't you Kelly? Let me write that down too so I don't forget. Okay, Mark, I need your approval right here, please."

6) Minimize the Problem Close:

In this close, the agent uses a calculator to reduce a large dollar amount to a ridiculously low daily amount. "Mark, I know how you feel. It's a little more than you wanted to pay. Let me ask you a question. If you could buy the home for only two dollars a day tomorrow, would you consider it? (Yes)

How long do you feel you'll be living in the home? Five years? You'll actually enjoy the home seven days a week, won't you? Or fifty weeks out of a year, if you take a two-week vacation? Only $2 a day x 7 days a week = $14 a week. 14 x 50 = $700 per year. $700 x 5 years = $3,500. Right? You can't afford not to buy it, can you? Shall we write it up then?"

Why Agents Need to Practice, Drill and Rehearse These Closes

There was once an agent named Bob who tried to use one of the above closes but didn't practice. The funny thing is that the customer knew it too. Many television sitcoms are built upon this type of premise, where the person faking it is found out, or has to fess up to it later. Ever see one of them? Let me tell you from experience, it's terribly embarrassing! Don't put yourself in that situation! Practice, drill and rehearse!

Why Don't Some Agents Practice These Techniques?

My belief is that many agents, especially new and/or part-time agents, have a tendency of wanting to be thought of as "nice" by their clients. They don't want to be thought of as a cheesy salesperson who tries to "sell" somebody something.

Selling somebody something is not perceived of as being cool.

It's like wearing a name-badge. Ever notice that when you wear a name-badge that some people treat you with sarcasm rather than respect? That's the way I feel when I wear one.

Since I've found that some people treat me with less respect when I wear a name badge, I don't like to wear one. Many agents feel a similar way about using memorized techniques on somebody. So if a client wants to write it up at $90,000, even if they know that $90,000 will never work, the "nice agent" will write it for $90,000. Why? Because they want to come across as being a "nice" salesperson. You can be nice, just don't be too easy.

Let me say it again. Be nice, but not easy. Practice using "Feel, Felt, Found," the six traditional closes, and information from your multi-list computer. Believe me, you'll look and sound more professional if you do and more like a weasel **if you don't practice!** And by practicing your selling techniques and using comparable sales data, you'll also help your clients make a more informed decision. And that's the proper definition of closing, isn't it? Because closing a sale is helping a client find a reason to make a decision. A decision they really want to make.

Before you can close any customer, you first have to gain their trust. That's what the next chapter is all about.

It's more important to do the right things than to be right about something.

— Bob Boog

Selling Homes 1-2-3

CHAPTER EIGHT
How to Gain Your Client's Trust

In almost 20 years of selling real estate, I've seen a lot of buyer's agents enter the real estate profession. Some have worked part-time, some full-time; some have been lucky and some have been not-so-lucky.

One thing I've noticed, however, is that intelligence is not an essential ingredient to being successful in selling homes. Friends, you can be as dumb as a stump and people will still buy from you. Even if you're new and work part-time.

Tom Hopkins has been saying this for years, and it still holds true today. **People will buy from you as long as they like you and trust you.**

In this chapter, I want to talk about ways to build trust with a client. How do you first get somebody to like and trust you?

By being honest. How else? By offering a sincere smile. Being genuinely interested in them. Using their name. By caring about people. By showing empathy for a person's situation. By selling yourself and your good qualities. By being a good listener. By establishing rapport. By finding out what the client really wants and helping him to get it. All of these are good answers.

The challenge is that in real estate, you can be the most honest person in town and can establish great rapport but if you don't have something good to show a client you can lose them as clients.

People in real estate have a problem because we don't always have the exact inventory available to show people what they want. Wouldn't it be great to have the perfect home to show to every client? Newly carpeted, freshly painted, and competitively priced?

Part of the challenge of real estate is to keep in touch with clients until something good rolls around. But sometimes we lose them before that happens, isn't this true? We want to show clients that we understand what they want but it just doesn't exist and they think you don't know what you're doing. As a result, they go somewhere else. The challenge is: how do we demonstrate to our clients that we truly respect them or understand their desires if what they want isn't available?

Pleasing the customer should be job one but sometimes we blow it because we try to convince somebody to buy something that they don't want, even though they may have said that it's what they wanted. It's not just when the client wants a pool home so we should just show them pool homes. It goes beyond that.

Let me give you another example of what I'm talking about, and see if this rings a bell with you.

When I first came into real estate I made an appointment to show homes to a buyer named Mr. Lee who happened to be Chinese. Over the phone, he told me that he wanted to buy a two-bedroom home. So I was prepared to show him two-bedroom homes. But when he came into the office that morning, he said that he wanted a three-bedroom home. And he wanted a large lot.

So what did I do? I panicked.

I threw out my entire list of two-bedroom homes, went to the multiple listing book, circled two or three listings, and then got in the car with him feeling kind of nervous.

Then do you know what I did? It still embarrasses me, but it's true. I brought Mr. Lee to a dirty, smelly, crappy old house.

I'd never even seen the inside of this home, but man was it a dog! Of course it fit Mr. Lee's price range, down payment and bedroom requirements to a tee, but oh man! What a dump! The people who used to live there I think were the Conehead family. After they took off in their spaceship, they left behind mass quantities of beer cans, garbage, and disgusting personal effects.

Then, here is the funny part. I looked up and smiled at Mr. Lee. The funniest thing about this story is that I actually thought that he might want to buy it. That's how naive I was. I mean it did have the right number of bedrooms, even though it was located next to Muley's Body Shop. Hey, it was in his price range. Right? It could happen.

Later when I learned that Mr. Lee had purchased a freshly painted, spotlessly clean two-bedroom in a nice neighborhood, I repeated the following mantra: "It's not fair. He told me he didn't want to buy a two-bedroom home and do you know what he did? He purchased a two-bedroom. He could have bought that home through me, that jerk!"

Has this ever happened to you before?

He could have bought
that home from me!

The point is: was it Mr. Lee's fault? No. Why should he have bought that clean two-bedroom home from me? Because I washed my car?

Think about it from his perspective. How did the first home I showed him make him feel?

Mr. Lee was probably thinking to himself: "That hot-shot buyer's agent with his brand-new car. He thinks I would want to live in a pig-sty! Why else would he bring me to one? I'm never letting him sell me a house!"

Is it any wonder that Mr. Lee never returned my calls? He lost his sense of trust with me on that first house.

Let's view the situation from another angle. Let's suppose that today you head to the local shopping mall to buy a pair of shoes. As you enter the shoe store, the sales person looks up, smiles and says: "Hi. May I help you?"

You answer: "Yes, I'd like a pair of shoes in this style." (You point to the style in a magazine advertisement.)

The salesperson winks. "I have just the ones for you." He disappears and returns with a box, and then he pulls out a dirty, old, smelly worn-out pair of shoes.

"These are nice, starter shoes," he or she says to you with a cheerful smile. "Try them on and tell me if you like them. They're a real steal too! Everybody just loves them!"

Now, what are you thinking as you slip on the pair of old shoes? Are you feeling happy as he does a hair flip with his freshly washed hair? Or are you seething inside. You're probably telling yourself: "I am never returning to this store!"

Question: Are you going to refer all your friends to that person? No. Why not?

Some people tell me: "Real estate is different. People don't care if the houses are dirty and smelly. Some people love to buy fixers."

Don't make me laugh. As Joan Rivers says: "Can we talk?"

I'm not talking about a contractor who's looking for a tear-down. A home that needs to be remodeled down to the studs with only one wall standing. Then after the inspector leaves the buyer has to tear down that wall too and remodel it.

I want you to be honest with yourself and think back to the times when people didn't call you back after showing homes. Why didn't they call you? Maybe they lost their trust in you.

I'm not proud of it, but it's happened to me. The dictionary defines trust as reliance. Confidence. Hope. Something entrusted. If I showed Mr. Lee a couple of junky homes last Saturday, why should he trust me with his house-buying decision this coming Saturday? Do you think he enjoys wasting time looking at smelly houses with me? No. He could have had more fun cleaning his sock drawer.

Some agents would argue: "Yeah, but Mr. Lee said that he wanted to buy a three-bedroom home. If you show him a clean two-bedroom home first then indirectly you're telling him that you don't respect his wishes. And the customer is always right, isn't he?"

76

The point isn't that you shouldn't listen to your customer. It's that you need to treat the customer with respect and dignity. Be concerned about his well-being. Indirectly, by showing the customer a clean home, you're telling the buyer that you respect him.

I respect you.

I sell homes in Los Angeles which is a melting pot of various ethnic communities. If Mr. Lee happens to be black and I tried to sell him a junky home, what might he think of me? Possibly that I'm a racist. That I'm saving the good houses for the white folks, right?

What if Mr. Lee happens to be Hispanic? Or if Mr. Lee is from India?

Their reactions will be the same. We're all human. We all want the best for our families. We're all suspicious of salespeople. We love to buy but we hate to be sold. Therefore, when I first meet Mr. Lee, I ask what is important to him in moving and I listen to him carefully. Hopefully I've got the perfect home. But if I don't have what he wants, I show him the cleanest house available. But if a clean house isn't available, I'm going to have him concentrate on *considering the neighborhoods* I show him.

Example "Mr. Lee, here is a list of homes that I pulled up from the computer. All of these are three-bedroom homes that are in your price range, but I've got to warn you, I haven't previewed all of them. I know that your time is valuable and so what I'd like to do today is just have you concentrate on choosing a desirable neighborhood. The first home I'd like to show you is a two-bedroom just to get your opinion on the neighborhood."

In other words, to gain a client's trust, when you are uncertain as to what the client truly wants, remember this surprisingly simple advice: **show a bitchin' home first.**

What you want to do is show them the best home in the best neighborhood first. I grew up in the '70's in Southern California so I call them "bitchin' homes". Show a bitchin' home first.

What Is A Bitchin' Home?

Bitchin' is slang for something or somebody beautiful and exciting. Surfers pronounce it "betch-en." When you show a bitchin' home to a buyer, they instinctively think two things. One: "I like this home." And two: "I like this real estate agent. He or she knows what I want and like. This home is bitchin'!"

The home may not be exactly what the buyer is looking for. But if the interior is clean, a buyer will think: "This sales-person thinks that I'm worthy of living in this quality home. He doesn't know that I live in a filthy roach-infested apart-ment." OR if the buyer is snooty, he will think: "Okay, not bad. At least the salesperson didn't show me a dump. Maybe I can work with this human to find this kind of home in a bet-ter neighborhood, if one is available."

Note: There is also a side benefit. When you show a bitchin' home, your buyer instinctively knows that you will show respect to his family and friends. You're their kind of agent!

Thank you!

Isn't that true? Buyers will instantly like you and trust you even if the next house you show them isn't as good. Even if the second home is a dog.

Now maybe in the past you were able to show a client two or three lousy houses then a good house, but nowadays you may not get that chance. People are getting busier and don't have time to waste. What happens if the first house is a dog, and as you and the client, Susan, are driving away, her beeper goes off. Susan says: "Can we find a phone? I need to make a call."

Then Susan uses your cell phone to return the call. She says, "Gee Bob, I'm sorry to cut this short but work just paged me and they really need me to come in today. Can we set up another time?"

Bob: "Sure Susan, no problem."

What happens next?

After she ducks my calls for the next month, I later discover that Susan and her husband bought that third house that I was planning to show them. Remember that "bitchin'" home that I thought they'd like? They liked it all right. I just never had a chance to show it to them.

Bob's Insider Advice: Show bitchin' homes first. Why? They help to develop trust especially if the home or property that the client wants is unavailable.

At this point, I'd like to spend some time on the importance of locating a neighborhood that your client will be happy to live in. Selecting the right neighborhood not only pleases the buyer, it also helps the agent sell more effectively. To learn more about this important insider selling technique, keep reading!

No one knows what he can do until he tries.

— Latin proverb

Selling Homes 1-2-3

CHAPTER NINE
Show Neighborhoods First

Dale Carnegie wrote: "The only way to get anybody to do anything is to get him to want to do it. That is the only way." Boy, is that statement true!

Question: What do most home-buyers want? What do they really, really want more than anything else?

Price? I used to think that a buyer always wanted to get the best price on a home. I thought that if I could show them the biggest, most inexpensive home on the market I'd make sales hand over fist. But after losing sales to buyers who purchased homes in completely different zip codes from where they said they wanted to live, I came to the realization that one has to assume that all buyers want to buy a home in the best neighborhood. They all want to live in a rich neighborhood like Beverly Hills so they can show off to their friends. Right? And that's not going to happen. So what do you do?

I think that the smart buyer's agent always assumes that the neighborhood matters more than anything else. **Find the neighborhood first and you will eliminate one-third of your showings.**

Your presentation might be: "What I'd like to do today, Jerry, is show you three homes in your price range that are located in three different neighborhoods. And I want you be honest and tell me how you feel about them. When we find the neighborhood that feels right for you, we can then concentrate on finding you the perfect house. Is that okay with you?"

This service approach is low-key and nonthreatening. Your apparent interest is only to find them the right neighborhood, and to most clients, this unassuming manner will build trust and score points.

Doesn't this contradict what was said in Chapter Eight? (Show a bitchin' home first?) Well, in a practical sense, sometimes it does. But what I'm trying to do is give you options on how to start out on the right foot with your client. Hopefully your bitchin' home will be in a possible "best neighborhood." If it's not, this becomes a judgment call. Sometimes you'll want to bring people to the home that looks bitchin' first to get them relaxed and on your wavelength. Other-times you'll want to take them to the best neighborhood first. You decide.

Why Is It Important to Show The Neighborhood First?

There are four surprisingly simple reasons why I recommend starting out by showing neighborhoods.

1) You may think a person is looking to buy a house, but some buyers are actually shopping for status or neighborhoods. They'd rather buy a brand neighborhood than a generic one. Things aren't always the way they seem, remember?

2) Showing neighborhoods first will cut down your showing time by almost one-third. In my city, there are usually about 30 homes priced from $210,000 to $235,000. These homes are found in five different neighborhoods. When I'm out showing homes with a client, I want to cover as much ground as possible. So if there are five neighborhoods, I know that my buyer is only going to really like one or possibly two of them. That means there will be three the buyer won't be interested in. So what do I do?

There's a four letter word for this . . . NEXT!

When I enter a neighborhood I'll ask the buyer if he likes it. If he doesn't, I don't even get out of the car, even if I'd called the seller in advance.

Bob: "How do you feel about this neighborhood Tony?"

Tony: "Too many cars parked in the street. I don't like it."

Bob: "No problem. There's a four letter word for this: Next!"

3) Showing neighborhoods first helps stretch the buyer's price range. When a potential purchaser loves a neighborhood there is no telling how high they'll go. I'll show as many homes as possible when a buyer says they like the neighborhood. Even ones that are over their price range. Why?

4) Because sometimes buyers don't tell the whole truth. Mom and dad might be willing to help out. Or a family member might co-sign. It took me awhile to figure this out. Eventually, however, I came to the conclusion that to some people price isn't the most important factor when buying a home.

Not too long ago I was showing houses to a single mom with three children. She told me that she could only afford $125,000. When I asked her why she wanted to move, she said: "I hate the place where I live." I believed her so I showed her one three-bedroom townhome in a nice neighborhood for $125,000 and a two-bedroom townhome in a slightly better neighborhood for $142,000. She asked to see a three bedroom, even though it was listed for $165,000 and loved it. Guess what happened next? Her father bought it and paid $160,000, *all cash*. Why? He wanted his grandchildren to grow up in a safe environment.

Here's another example. Monty and Joy wanted to buy a home in my city. When asked why they wanted to move, Monty told me: "We need at least a 1,500 square-foot home, but we can go no higher than $165,000. By the way, Bob, we'd also like a safe neighborhood where our children can walk to school."

Which do you think I keyed on, the price, the square footage or the neighborhood? Clue: Remember the rule, show neighborhoods first?

Knowing that finding the right neighborhood will help build trust, I pulled up to a smaller, slightly more expensive home than the one they said they wanted. This home was listed for $172,000 and was located one block away from a school in the world's safest neighborhood.

I've seen enough!

After I showed them the inside, Monty told me that they wanted to purchase it. "I've seen enough. Let's write it up," he said.

In private Monty confessed the truth to me. He said that his son Mikey had gotten beaten up at school by bullies; however with Mikey in the car, Monty didn't want to discuss the matter with me.

Why did Monty tell me this in private? He felt that he could trust me. I showed him something he liked. Monty was shopping for a neighborhood even though I thought he wanted to buy a larger house! Things aren't always what they seem to be, right?

Has something like this ever happened to you? Sure.

In the past, you wouldn't have figured it out. You would have shown Monty all of the homes in his price range and he still wouldn't have bought. Then a more experienced agent would have sold Monty the smaller, slightly more expensive home in the better neighborhood.

By showing neighborhoods first, I was able to pinpoint what Monty and Joy wanted with only one showing. Luck? You'll see how much luckier you'll be when you use this idea.

It's been this way in the past, it's this way in the present, and it will remain the same in the future. That's what real estate gurus mean when they say, "There are three things to remember when buying real estate: location,

location, location." Whether it's the school system, prestige or safety, many people would rather purchase a smaller home in a great neighborhood, than a larger house in a lousy neighborhood.

Bob's insider advice: Find the neighborhood first, then locate the house, even if the house costs more than what the client says he can afford, and you'll find yourself making more sales!

Now, you can't sell a house without a buyer. How do you find them? You'll find out in the next chapter.

"No matter what you sell, **you** make a difference. There are nearly 2000 life insurance companies offering the same products; all stockbrokers selling listed securities have the same stocks and bonds to sell; real estate agents sell multiple-listed properties...What it all boils down to is, you must sell yourself. The prospect must like you and believe in you. If not, there is no reason anyone should buy from you instead of someone else."

—Joe Girard *Closing the Sale Every Time*

Selling Homes 1-2-3

CHAPTER TEN
Finding Buyers

You know that in order for people to buy from you they have to like you and trust you. Agreed? Okay. And in order for people to like you and trust you, they have to get to know you.

You could be the greatest salesperson in all of Southern California, or in the entire eastern half of North America, but unless you go out and meet people, nobody's going to know that you're this warm, wonderful person.

Why don't we like to meet new people?

> 1) We're lazy.
>
> 2) We're afraid.
>
> 3) We feel that we're bothering them.

I don't know about your area of the country, but in Southern California, it's not unusual for migrant workers to wait outside hardware stores looking for manual day-jobs. Homeowners regularly hire them to help with fix-it projects around the house. One day I drove by a group of these men. Four of the fellows were sitting on the curb and three were standing up. Of the three standing up, one man made eye contact with me, then started jumping up and down and waving his arms wildly. The other two guys had their hands in their pockets and were looking down the road.

Which person do you think caught my attention first? Who do you think I hired? The ones sitting down, the men with their hands in their pockets or that wild-man enthusiastically waving his arms?

I think that most buyers and sellers think about us real estate people much the same way. Some of us are sitting at the curb, tired and bored. Others of us seem disinterested, but some of us are waving our arms wildly at every opportunity, trying to make something happen.

Now I understand that some buyer's agents have had a bad experience with prospecting. And that is why some have decided to become buyer's agents or buyer's assistants.

One guy told me on a job interview. "I'm a buyer's agent and I don't take listings. I don't prospect. I've done all the bad-pizza phone-blitz nights. I've doorknocked till my knuckles had blisters. Nothing worked. I don't prospect."

"Do you go back and visit your past clients?" I asked.

"No. I've got my own selling system," he said. "I put classified ads in the paper that work miracles. I made $30,000 in the last six months." Not bad.

Guess what? I didn't hire him. I figured if his past clients didn't want him coming around there must be something wrong with him. Besides, I already had a secretary answering the phones.

If you are new in real estate, my attitude may seem strange to you. But you have to understand that I work mainly on referrals. And if you can't go back to the people who purchased homes from you and ask them for more business, you must not have done a very good job with them.

What if you just can't bear to see your old clients, what then? Here are five ideas for you.

One: Once a month, hire somebody to mail a postcard for you!

Two: Then call the people on your mailing list and ask if they received your mailing piece!

Three: Pay somebody to drive small gifts to all your past clients with one of your business cards attached to the present. Example: giving all the women clients flowers for Mother's Day.

Four: Hire somebody to pass out a prospecting flyer for an upcoming open house to fifty surrounding neighbors.

Five: Then hold the open house on the date promised.

Why not? Somebody has to keep your name out there. Woody Allen is quoted as saying "90% of success is just showing up." I believe that 99% of prospecting is *just being consistent.*

Because some of us are "binge" prospectors. We go to extremes. I had one agent who would send out 500 newsletters once a year. Every four months he'd doorknock 100 homes. Another agent would make 100 phone calls for the year. This was his favorite saying: *"This prospecting stuff doesn't work."*

What many agents have found to be true is that successful prospecting is like the old Chinese water-torture technique. Little by little you drip-drip-drip on people's foreheads until they finally get the message and call you. So figure out what kind of prospecting you like to do, and then do it on a consistent basis.

Bob's insider advice: Be consistent in prospecting. Don't go to extremes.

I think another problem that some agents have with prospecting is a negative connotation with the word. Maybe you need to think of it as networking. If you were invited to a dinner party at the White House tomorrow, and you didn't know anybody there, what would you do? You'd sit down and introduce yourself to the people sitting at your table, wouldn't you? You would say, "Hi, my name is Joe Shmoe and I'm in real estate. What do you do?"

That's called networking.

But isn't that really what we do when we go prospecting?

Ten years ago, I took out a new person out to do some prospecting. We each left my car with 60 promotional pieces to hang on doors and we planned to meet in one hour to compare notes.

Sixty minutes later we returned and I had only three doorhangers left. Cynthia, the new agent had 54 left over. "What happened?" I asked. "You started out with 60 doorhangers. You only passed out six in one hour?"

"I'm sorry," she apologized, "but I started gabbing with the second woman I met and she had a friend who was interested in buying a house up the street. So I walked up the street with her friend and showed her the inside of the house. She loved it. By the time I got back, I only had time to talk to five other people, but I did manage to get three more phone numbers!"

You want to know something? I buzzed through those apartments and passed out fifty-seven doorhangers and to this day nobody called me! Zero. Zilch. Nothing. Nada. Cynthia made a sale.

Question: Who was prospecting or networking the right way? Bob the busy bumblebee, running through the neighborhood flinging flyers at every porch, avoiding every homeowner who might want to talk to me, or smiling Cynthia who stopped to chat and smile with everyone? I think you know the answer.

Cynthia acts like a gracious hostess to everyone. She puts names in her database and calls people at night to see if they received her invitation to attend her open house. Is it any wonder she managed to sell four homes in one month? She even gives out her business cards when she goes shopping at the mall.

Does that experience hit home with you?

I mean for years I'd heard that old adage, "Real estate is a numbers game." **Yet how many people like to be considered just another number?** If you're one of them, raise your hand. The guys in the white jackets will take you somewhere nice and quiet.

Friends, real estate is also a referral game.

And people will gladly send you referrals if they like you. But you have to let them in. You have to consistently press the flesh. You have to consistently contact people, mail them postcards and keep in touch.

Your main job, if you are new in real estate, is to go out and meet people each day and have them like you.

It's that simple. It doesn't have to be new people either; it can be family and friends. The people from your old job. Did you know that the top salespeople spend three or four hours every day meeting and re-meeting people? It's like they're running for a political office.

"But I don't like to doorknock," agents tell me. If you are new in real estate or working part-time, just send out a mailing piece. Send it to friends from your old job. Then call them up to see if they got it. On the weekends, go to see people at garage sales. Not to buy stuff, but to meet people and get their vitals: names, addresses and phone numbers. Bring a handful of business cards and have some fun! Think of some other ideas but at least send out some mail once a day. Twenty people everyday for five days a week equals one hundred new people. **(5 x 20 = 100)** Or five "just a note" cards x five days = 25 contacts a week. **(5 x 5 = 25 per week, x 4 = 100 per month).**

Remember, the secret is to be consistent and to have people like you. You want people to remember you as being a nice person who would be perfect to work with their family. Not some hot-shot agent who seems snooty and too

Sorry, I'm too good for you.

good for them.

I can remember one time walking door to door, and when the door opened, a miniature collie was headed straight for my throat. I happened to be holding a clipboard in my hands, and without thinking, I used it to whack the dog. I honestly thought the dog was going to bite me! The dog yelped and rolled over three times before he started to yap at me. Yap, yap, yap.

The homeowner, an elderly woman, saw everything. She was horrified at what I'd done, and told me off something good. Man, she bent my ear for a good ten minutes, easy. What did I do? I stood there, and listened, and listened, and listened. I tried to apologize but she wouldn't let me. After a little while she invited me inside, and apologized for talking so much. She even gave me a drink of water before I left so I sent her a thank-you note.

This might sound corny, but about four months later, I got a telephone call. The voice on the other line said, "Are you the man who hit my dog with the clipboard?"

"Yes ma'am," I answered somewhat nervously.

"This is Mrs. Echols. I'm thinking about selling, and I'd like you to come on over. I'm going to list with you."

Why me, the dog batterer? Plain and simple. She said she liked me.

Remember: You don't **have to** doorknock, telephone canvas or mail people postcards. You can join community service groups, the Chamber of Commerce, the Jaycees, or professional organizations. You can get people to like you anywhere you go. The key is to like other people and they'll like you.

Seek Out Different Angles While Following Up

If you're persisting with the same thing over and over again, you become annoying and people can't wait to get rid of you. Isn't that true? One agent I know offers a **free dinner for two** for people who attend his open houses. While at the open house, he meets everybody with a big smile and afterwards files their names, addresses and phone numbers in his database. Then he holds a drawing for the winner and contacts everybody to let them know who won. Then he contacts them later with information about recent sales or new listings.

His famous phrase is "I never send out a single mailing piece unless I've got that person's phone number. You're wasting your money if you're presumptuous enough to think that people will ever call you."

Another buyer's agent visits commercial offices and gives

free stuff to all the receptionists. He takes their business cards and sends the receptionists notes in the mail. Why? The receptionists all seem to know who just had a baby and who just got a raise, don't they? Another buyer's agent faxes notes to all the accountants and divorce attorneys in town and then he calls on them with free gift baskets. See where I'm going with this? You probably have some ideas of your own. We all have our own approaches, sensitivities, weaknesses and methods of communication.

People out there are dying to meet you! And when you increase the value of someone else's existence, you increase the value of your own existence. What does it take? A smile. A look of understanding. A kind word. A handshake.

Right now, you probably have some great ideas on what you can do. Like the Nike slogan says: Just do it! And **be consistent** about doing it!

A person who thinks his job is important receives mental signals on how to do his job better; and a better job means more promotions, more prestige and more happiness.

—David J. Schwartz, *The Magic of Thinking Big*

CHAPTER ELEVEN
Don't Be Too Ingratiating

The word "ingratiate" means to gain favor or acceptance through deliberate effort. What I mean by "don't be too ingratiating" is **don't flatter buyers too much**. In sales we have to charm clients some of the time. Right? We often laugh at the buyer's jokes, and indulge their opinions, attitudes and concerns. And of course we admire their intelligent home-purchasing decisions!

Yes, you can agree with a buyer, but don't overdo it!

Now if you disagree on some minor points, you'll be fine. Buyers will find you to be intelligent and perceptive. But if you agree on everything too blatantly, people will think less of you. They'll think you're trying to hustle them. They'll be reminded of Eddie Haskell with his smarmy smile and insincere flattery. Imagine Eddie Haskell showing a home:

Eddie: "Gee, doesn't this kitchen look incredibly beautiful, Mrs. Cleaver?"

Good old Eddie, he's oilier than a kerosene lamp. Just as June Cleaver was able to see right through Eddie's "charm", your buyer will be able to see through your insincerity.

I remember once when I was new I had just learned Tom Hopkins' technique on using "tie-down" questions. I was so proud. I must have used twelve tie-downs on my client in a row. Every chance I got I was making an observation and following it with a "isn't it?" "doesn't it?" or "wasn't it?" "This home shows pride of ownership, doesn't it?" "This living room sure looks spacious, doesn't it?" Finally my client stopped me. She said, "Lighten up Bob, you're scaring me. You sound just like a robot."

Then about two years ago, a similar thing happened. By then I was a broker and I was accompanying a part-time agent while she showed homes to her buyer. Oh, oh, something about what I was experiencing seemed very familiar. Every time we would pull up in front of a property, she would say: "This neighborhood shows pride of ownership, doesn't it?"

One time when she said it, there were a number of men standing around, drinking beer in front of the garage next door. They were definitely giving off a negative vibe. You know the type: intimidating-looking guys with shaved heads, angry scowls and colorful tattoos decorating their muscular chests. I was a little worried and looked at the buyer sitting in the back seat. Her eyes were as wide as saucers. She didn't want to get out of the car and I didn't blame her. I didn't want to get out either!

My point is don't say things just to practice techniques. When somebody says something phony, you know what happens? After a while you don't trust that person. So remember: use tie-down questions after the client has expressed some interest in a feature. If you use too many tie-downs, it will cause a client to dislike you or distrust you. It may even drive a person crazy.

Be honest. Be sincere.

If you're going to try to charm your buyer, do it right. Only say things you can deliver with feeling. If you're not genuine, the client will see right through it.

Oh I love how they've used those black hippie beads, don't you?" Right.

If you don't personally like a property, keep your thoughts to yourself. Even if you have to flick a cockroach or two off the mini-blinds in order to open them. Hey, it may be the very home that your client adores!

It's funny but when I was new in real estate I tried to be too helpful. Too observant. Ever do that? I would try to top the client's complaint." Here's an example of how dumb I was:

Client: "These bedrooms are just too small."

Bob: "What about that tiny kitchen? And that bathroom! Did you see the mold in the shower? How can people live like that? Somebody should call the Health Department on those people!"

Client: "A moldy shower? I didn't even see that. Still the yard is nice, and it has a four-car garage. I really liked that garage."

Bob: "Yes, but this home belongs to the Helmers Elementary School, not Meadows. Everybody knows that Meadows is better than Helmers."

Client: "Oh really? How interesting."

Cut to two weeks later:

Bob: "So of all the three hundred and fifty homes we've seen thus far, which did you feel most comfortable in?"

Client: "We both really like that one with the moldy shower and the four-car garage on Littlefield Drive, but of course we'd never want to buy it. We want our children to go to Meadows School. Remember? You said that Meadows was better than Helmers. Remember?"

Bob: "Yes, well, Helmers is still a fine school. What are we talking about? You two don't even have any children yet."

Client: "That's okay. We'll just wait until something else comes up. We have plenty of time. We're not in any hurry."

Did this strike a nerve with anybody? My face turned red in embarrassment over that one for a long time. **Lesson: if you can't be positive, don't dwell on the negatives of a property.**

I've noticed that smart agents dwell on the positives but still notice details. But if your clients can't think of anything good to say, don't add to their negativity. On the other hand, buyers will like you and trust you more if you point out a legitimate concern. For example, you may notice that the ceiling shows signs of leakage or that there are plumbing problems in the bathroom. These items should be disclosed and you owe it to the purchaser to point out these defects. If your client asks you a question about a defect and you honestly don't know whether it's a problem, just answer them truthfully with "I don't know, but I'll make it a point to find out for you." Then find it out for them.

Smart agents have a good eye for detail. They watch the reactions of a buyer when he or she enters a room, they ask how long they've been looking, and if they feel comfortable in the neighborhood.

If your buyers say they don't like the neighborhood, don't press, even if you personally like the home or the sellers. Why? Because if your buyers don't like the neighborhood, 99% of the time they're not going to buy the home. That's why I think that you can afford to tell people it's okay to think about it — as long as you stay in constant communication with them.

Sometimes, however, you do need to use pressure. The buyers like the home and the neighborhood, and the listing agent tells you that Betty at Jonestown Realty is writing an offer on it. You believe that the listing agent is being truthful. But no matter how hard you try to convince Ryan and Isabel that they had better act now, they refuse to budge. Let me let you in on a secret. *Sometimes buyers are more afraid of making a bad choice than making a good choice and they have to lose a house before they'll buy one.* Got that? Sometimes you have to lose in order to win.

Floyd Wickman has a saying that goes: "Fear of loss is oftentimes a greater motivator than benefits gained." I think he's right.

What about this one. Have you ever gotten too enthusiastic about a home before the client has seen it? Ever do that?

"Kathy and Lou, you're going to love this home! I mean, it is so bitchin', it's out of this world!"

Be careful about pre-selling a home, even if you are being sincere. It can backfire on you. If the client doesn't like the home, he'll think that you're not on the same wave-length as him. Then you might lose him as a client.

"You call this gorgeous? This is the worst home I've ever seen. It got hit with an ugly stick!"

Whatever.

Don't give buyers ammunition to be negative. Try a modest approach that still sounds positive.

"This next home has a spacious backyard and seems light and bright to me, Roxana. Tell me how you feel about it."

Try it and see how it works for you.

A Tip for Selling Condo's

Upper Units usually have EVEN Unit numbers.
Lower units are usually ODD Numbered.

To easily remember this: HEAVEN is an UPPER unit so it's an EVEN number.

Whenever you meet a person with a big ego, feed the ego.

— Bob Boog

Selling Homes 1-2-3

MULTIPLE OFFERS PROCEDURE

Date of offer:_____ **Address:**_____

Buyer name:_____**Sales agent:**_____

_____By placing his initials here, the seller for the above mentioned property hereby acknowledges receiving notification from the listing agent that multiple offers for the purchase of this property have been presented. In order to ensure that ALL purchasers are treated fairly, seller requests that ALL SELLING AGENTS acknowledge the bottom of this instruction and return by fax to the listing agent. By doing so, selling agent agrees to inform purchaser of the following:

Inform all parties that there are multiple offers.
1) Each interested party is requested to submit their "best" offer in writing to the listing agent no later than:_____.
2) Seller will accept or provide a counter offer ONLY to the offer which the Seller determines to be the "best" offer to him.
3) In the event the first choice of the "best" offer does not result in an accepted purchase agreement, Seller will accept or provide a counter offer ONLY to the offer which Seller determines to be the "next best offer" and so on.
4) In the event the first accepted purchase agreement does not result in a closed escrow, listing agent will notify all selling agents of the previously submitted offers that the property is once again available, and will invite new offers.

As Selling Agent, I hereby acknowledge receipt of this multiple offers procedure agreement, and agree to return by FAX to the listing agent WHETHER OR NOT MY PURCHASER IS WILLING TO CHANGE THEIR ORIGINAL PURCHASE CONTRACT.

_____   _____
LISTING AGENT   SELLING AGENT

_____   _____
DATE SIGNED   DATE SIGNED

CHAPTER TWELVE
How To Skillfully Read Buyers

When I first started out in real estate, I was at a disadvantage when working with buyers. I didn't know that much about financing, I hadn't memorized all the homes on the market, and I wasn't very good at reading people. Now I think that to be successful when you're one-on-one with a buyer, you have to be like a quarterback who knows how to read the defense. You have to know how to read people. For example, some people won't say a word when they don't like a home, right? Some people don't want to open up. They just cross their arms.

But we're supposed to know that they didn't like the home! Right?

I didn't know that. See when I was new I had a tendency to live in Fantasy Land. I went around believing what people told me. Because that's how I operated. If you said, for example, that you didn't like two-story houses, I wouldn't show you any two-story homes. I didn't know that there were people who would say one thing but end up doing the opposite.

Hey, I had some people tell me that they didn't want a pool home and guess what they ended up purchasing? A pool home. I had somebody else tell me that they didn't want a two-story house. Guess what they bought? A two-story.

This kind of thing used to drive me crazy until I discovered a secret. If you want to skillfully read a buyer, just remember this saying: **buyers are like birds.**

Some people think I'm crazy when I say this, but I think it's true!

Scientists have shown that many human decisions can be influenced by what is called "the herd mentality," and most listing agents have found this to be true. Within a week after a "for sale" sign goes up in a neighborhood, for example, another family often gets the itch to move. Before you know it, four new signs go up the neighborhood!

There was a bank in Singapore that experienced a crowd of people withdrawing their money in a frenzy. Yet the institution was strong and solvent. Why were the people making a run on the bank? It turned out that a bus strike had caused an unusually large amount of people to crowd outside the bank waiting for the next bus to come. People driving by, however, saw this large, unruly crowd and assumed that there must be something bad going on inside the bank. The people who withdrew their money did so because of the herd mentality.

We know that when it comes to selling homes, people like to follow the herd, but what about when purchasing a home? What happens then?

The "Birds of a Feather" Syndrome

Have you ever heard the proverb, "birds of a feather flock together"? It's another version of the herd mentality, isn't it? People will drive around a neighborhood and notice the people, the schools, the cars parked in the street and then they'll decide whether or not they'd like to join the flock of birds that are living there.

Over the years I have noticed that there seemed to be a lot of truth to the birds of a feather saying! So much so, that I took it one step further and even identified some of the common bird/buyers that populate the real estate market in my community.

Perhaps this method of analyzing buyers may help you to become more effective with selling homes in your neck of the woods. Maybe it won't, but keep reading and see for yourself.

PLEASE UNDERSTAND that when I say that birds of a feather flock together I'm not talking about steering people: sending people away from a particular neighborhood for discriminatory purposes. What I'm talking about is listening to what the client is saying, much like a forest ranger listens to birds singing in the forest.

If I were to take a hike in the woods with Ranger Jim, for example, he might suddenly stop and say: "Listen."

After pausing for a moment, I might hear a bird calling in the distance.

Ranger Jim: "Did you hear that meadowlark?"

Bob: "How can you tell it's a meadowlark without seeing it?"

Ranger Jim: "Because of its distinctive call. Listen!"

Now, some forest rangers are so talented that they can actually cup their hands and mimic the call of the bird. Ever see that happen? Guess what? If you practice, you'll be able to communicate better with the birds/buyers that live in your community, just by learning what hot buttons appeal to them.

Here's what I mean. When a client calls me in response to an ad in the newspaper, I'll listen to what he or she tells me and then I'll often try to identify what kind of bird he or she is. Sometimes I've laid out birdseed (i.e., words in the ad) to attract a specific kind of bird, so when I ask what ad he or she is responding to, I may already have a good idea as to what kind of bird I might be dealing with.

Next I'll assign the buyer to one of the five groups that I'm about to profile. Then finally I'll see if I can show this bird homes in neighborhoods where I think he'll feel comfortable. Again, it is a violation of the law to steer a prospective buyer either into or away from a neighborhood for discriminatory purposes. I want you to be perfectly clear on that matter because it isn't what I'm referring to when I talk about the "Birds of a feather" syndrome.

The color, age, race, familial status or sex of the bird isn't important. It's what the bird wants or says he wants that gives me a clue to his or her identity. Now my city might be composed of different groups than yours, so have fun with these bird categories. Remember that your area may have groups of birds that are unique to your community. You might have Inner-City-Birds, Ranch-Birds, Military-Base Birds or Senior-Citizen Birds. I'm not trying to be John Audubon here; the idea is to just get you thinking about your local market. Who lives where you do?

Here are the five groups of birds that inhabit my city:
1) The Sexy Single Bird
2) The All-American Bird
3) The Yuppie Bird
4) The Executive Bird
5) The Eclectic Bird. Now let me describe the distinctive features of each bird group.

1) THE SEXY SINGLE BIRD

This bird feels young, even though he or she may not be chronologically young. Age doesn't matter. These buyers perceive themselves as youthful, attractive and sexy, and they like to wear clothes and drive cars that tell the world that they feel this way. They can be physically disabled, newly divorced, single, or recently married: **familial status doesn't matter**. They just look and act like they're in a dating mode!

Bob's Insider Advice: When selling homes to sexy singles, use words that evoke images of sex or love, because that is their true hot button. For example, words such as cute, sexy, passionate, gorgeous, romantic, lovely, adorable, beautiful, favorite, darling, new, springtime, fresh, and hot will appeal to them.

You have to be careful to avoid running foul of fair housing laws so always check the local ordinances in your area before advertising.

One time I listed a property that I felt would appeal to a sexy-single buyer so when I wrote the advertisement, I used a headline that read: SEXY HOT TUB! The rest of the ad was: "This hot-looking 2 bedroom Townhome screams out passion and romance! The sizzling hot tub will add spice to your sex life! Now only $80,250!"

A few days later, I received a call from a man who sounded like he was in his mid-twenties. When I showed him the complex I noticed that he wasn't wearing a wedding ring, he kept checking his hair in the mirror and he flirted with a buxom girl sitting out by the pool. Two days before escrow closed, I was surprised to discover that he was almost 40, married and had two young children! This sale taught me

that many sexy-single birds aren't necessarily single!

Most sexy-single birds in my area are fond of buying townhouses and condominiums. Do you have any sexy singles where you live?

2) THE ALL-AMERICAN BIRD

All-American Birds are traditionalists. If it's a guy, he's normally a friendly, family man who likes to change his own oil and mow the lawn himself. He prefers to work from 9:00 to 5:00 during the week, kick back on weekends and watch the Super Bowl. His hobbies often include outdoor activities, such as playing softball, camping or jetskiing. Many times, the All-American Bird female is a full-time homemaker, or she is active with the PTA but this is not always the case.

The All-American bird believes that having a decent job and owning a home in a neighborhood where the streets are safe and the children can walk to school is achieving the American dream. Many of these birds, both male and female are union people, work for large companies, or are employed by the county, city or state governments. "I'd rather be fishing" or "Union proud" is a common bumper sticker found on their American-built vehicles.

All-American Birds are members of all races, sexes, religions, familial status and national origins. Some are young, and some are old. They include the blind and physically challenged too.

All-Americans enjoy the simple pleasures of life and are oftentimes the nicest people to deal with because they are sincere and down to earth. An ad that might attract an All-American Bird would be:

CLEAN OZZIE & HARRIET HOME
or
"LEAVE IT TO BEAVER" NEIGHBORHOOD
Traditional home on quiet tree-lined street.
Value galore.
Walk to schools. 3 bedrooms 2 bath.
Only $125,000!

Bob's Insider Advice: most All-American buyers place a high value on safety, security, cleanliness, godliness and tradition. Hot buttons include: Mom, America, hot dogs, stability, Fourth of July, value, safety, "Leave it to Beaver," heritage, apple pie, conventional, baseball, traditional and secure.

An All-American-couple will probably nod their heads when you say the following phrase at the right house: "Tim and Rebecca, I can almost imagine you guys, a few months from now, sitting out here in the backyard on the Fourth of July, eating hot dogs, drinking cold sodas, and watching the fireworks, can't you?"

Do you have any All-Americans living in your neck of the woods?

3) THE YUPPIE BIRD

A Yuppie Bird is not necessarily young or white, though most aspire to be upwardly mobile. This bird may also be older, and can be African-American, Asian, Arabic or from just about any ethnic group or country of origin. Although some Yuppies have children, most are working professionals who are **not** interested in having children. They may already have a child who is now in his or her late teens, or they may have children spend a weekend with them, but normally these birds are mainly focussed on their career.

Brand names are important to the Yuppie Bird. Why? Because in this age of information overload, Yuppie Birds use brand names as a short cut to decision making. Most Yuppies would prefer to wear the latest designer label shirt than the generic brands. In their minds, the brand name is a quick route to quality. A Yuppie Bird will notice your choice of brands too, so better put on a Polo shirt, a sweater from Nordstrom's or wear your Nike shoes when dealing with a Yuppie Bird. By doing so, you're conveying the impression that you understand and appreciate the Yuppie's value system. You're on the same wavelength as them.

Pets are also a priority and you'd better treat their animals like family members because Yuppies do. Privacy is also key. A quiet location or a garden is often a big selling factor. Snob appeal can also be a plus. And because Yuppie Birds often travel, a small low-maintenance yard often makes them happy. They may have previously owned a family mansion in the past, so yard work is generally not keen with them. Garden: yes, yard work: no.

Then again, some Yuppies hire help. They'll pay a gardener so don't totally discount a large yard either.

Obviously each individual Yuppie Bird will have his or her own needs. What's interesting about Yuppies is that many will want homes larger than they really need. A Yuppie Bird will insist, for example, on having a three-bedroom home when it's only a single man occupying the home. I think it's because many Yuppies take their career so seriously that they need an office where they can work at home. And to some Yuppies, the house is a reflection of their egos. (Oftentimes people with gigantic egos require spacious homes as well.)

Yuppie Birds crave privacy, so don't show them homes where other people can look down on them. Instead, show a Yuppie a house on a hilltop with a breathtaking view.

Bob's Insider Advice: Yuppie Birds are often very demanding, affluent buyers and many are quite computer literate. Keep checking your e-mail! If you cater to their needs, they will tell the world about you.

Here are some yuppie-bird hot buttons: Privacy, ultra-modern, view, quality, tasteful, value, neat-as-a-pin, designer brand, top-notch, snob, Number 1, professional, pristine, adult occupied, entertainer's delight, new, novel, showplace, private, and secluded.

Again, be careful how you advertise. You don't want to be seen as discriminatory towards blind people, for example, because you advertised a view home. Check your local fair housing council for their guidelines as to what is acceptable and what is not.

4) THE EXECUTIVE BIRD

Mr. or Ms. Executive Bird is often a former Yuppie Bird who now has two children and a dog. Executive Birds are usually upper middle-class in income and some are snobbish. However, unlike Yuppies, their lives normally revolve around the needs of their children. Therefore most Executives want a spacious home in the best neighborhood for their children. These are the soccer-moms of the world with their Dodge Caravans chauffeuring a team off to practice. Oftentimes both husband and wife work, so daycare provider questions will be asked if they do have children.

Unlike All-Americans, however, Executive Birds sometimes have nannies or live-in helpers to watch the children, so they may be looking for a separate bathroom/shower for the caretaker. An Executive Bird without children is not afraid of making changes and will sell or buy at the drop of a hat if the deal is right. Creative financing is never a problem as the Executive will call on his or her own army of experts before reaching a decision.

Most Executive Birds want or demand to have a family room or place to showcase their awards. They also like places with lots of storage and a decent-sized yard. Many have a belief about "he who dies with the most toys wins." So three-car garages and spacious closets are features of great interest.

Do you have anything bigger?

Executive Birds are competitive people. Money, success and recognition motivate them, and they are often extremely concerned about what other people think. It's wise to let them browse through a pre-purchase booklet filled with information about the local area, past satisfied customers, points of interest and school information.

Many Executive Birds are take-charge types who will visit the local schools without telling you and will even talk to neighbors before they purchase, so avoid making off-the-cuff comments without checking your facts. If you make a mistake with this buyer, the error may come back to haunt you for a long time.

Bob's Insider Advice: Executive Birds like to "keep up with the Jones family". They adore new gadgets, dining at high-priced restaurants, and attending movie premieres just to be the first one to do so. Many will compare notes with your tastes. Be careful with recommendations you give them. You'll hear the story about the painter who does inferior work for a long time.

Most of the hot buttons that work with a Yuppie Bird can also attract an Executive. It's just that the Executive is a bit more concerned with living near a prestigious school than having total privacy. Better words and phrases to use with an Executive Bird might be: Safety, quality, pride, prestige, showplace, executive, professional, close to school, winner, family, pleasing, lovely, new, blue-ribbon, modern and award-winning.

Don't hesitate to ask for referrals from this buyer. Executives love to make recommendations and have influence over people. Most love to be in control.

5) THE ECLECTIC BIRD

The Eclectic Bird is the quirky buyer who usually wants something that nobody else wants: the under-maintained house with the worn green carpet, the non-conforming property filled with the fragrance of incense, the tiny house with the beautiful tree in the backyard. He or she isn't always "artsy" but the typical Eclectic Bird does have an independent streak. Some Eclectics have really made it in life and don't believe in wearing any trappings of success. They'll buy only the property that they feel is suitable for them, so not every property has to have bells tinkling like some temple in Tibet.

Many Eclectic Birds like to travel and some would rather backpack than take a bus. New-age parents, health fanatics, authors, environmentalists, psychic readers and celebrities all seem to fall into this category. Most of these people enjoy a challenge, so don't be afraid to give them what they want, even if it isn't perfectly cleaned and polished.

The true Eclectic Bird loves properties that only suit **their** special needs. The "king of pop", Michael Jackson, is a perfect example of an Eclectic Bird. He has the financial capacity to buy whatever he wants, and if you tell him about

a 120-acre ranch atop Mt. Fuji, the mansion that nobody else wants to buy, he might eagerly snap it up. Eclectic Birds are like that. They want what nobody else wants. The funky stuff.

Ironically many poor people, like the *Cratchit* family in the book, *The Christmas Carol* by Charles Dickens, also fit this role. A property can be a shack in the worst neighborhood that nobody else wants to buy but then a poor-but-honest hardworking man with vision signs the paperwork. His budget only allows him to qualify for a $45,000 loan, and when the seller approves the ridiculously low price, guess what? You've just made a sale to an Eclectic Bird. Congratulations!

Eclectic Birds are found in the very highest priced homes, the extreme lows of the housing markets, and the quirky cracks in between.

Hot button words include: Charm, quirky, funky, different, well-being, privacy, inspired, without equal, incomparable, artsy, writer's home, apart, well-built, crafted and unique.

Bob's Insider Advice: If you or your clients have been discriminated call the Housing Discrimination Hotline: 1-800-669-9777.

SOME FURTHER THOUGHTS ON BIRD-WATCHING

Finding a way to read buyers to determine where they might want to buy is an art, not a science. If you put a little bit of effort into using this system, you might find that it saves you time and effort. It gives you a hook to use if you are having difficulty figuring out what exactly it is that your buyer wants.

Now there are other methods to read people, and this bird method may or may not work for you. A famous psychologist distinguished certain people as expressives, analyticals and dominants. If using that system works for you, terrific. Use it.

I use the Birds of a Feather System because the buyer usually tells me what kind of bird he or she is. How does the buyer tell me?

One: The lender must pre-qualify the bird based on factual income data submitted by my buyer. When you combine the income documentation with a "quickie" credit report, our price range is usually going to be very accurate. That narrows the search parameters to a fairly specific price range, doesn't it?

Two: When I take out a buyer, I show them neighborhoods first. Once the buyer selects the neighborhood, I work the system backward to figure out what kind of bird he or she is. If he's a sexy single, I might start noticing "hot corvettes" or other things that I think we might have in common. Pretty soon I'll be talking his language! For example: Tom is prequalified up to $300,000, and I think that he might be a Yuppie Bird or an All-American. I show him a bitchin' home in a Yuppie neighborhood and one in an All-American neighborhood. To my surprise, Tom says that he likes the All-American neighborhood best, even though the house costs only $255,000 and he qualifies for much more.

Question: What kind of bird is Tom?

Answer: He's an All-American. So if Tom likes an All-

American neighborhood, I let him tell me about his last hunting or fishing trip. Pretty soon, he purchases what he wants and not what I think he should want. In other words, I let my client choose the neighborhood that he or she wants to live in.

Here's a mistake that many new people and part-time agents often make. The lender will qualify a buyer higher than what the buyer may want to spend and the new agent tries to stretch a buyer into a home that they don't want to buy. Why? Because the lender gave a high amount and **the agent** likes the home. I may love that home for $300,000, but Tom may not. Or Tom might be more interested in saving for his retirement or investing in the stock market.

The point is to listen to your buyer. He or she has to make the payment every 30 days, not you. There may be a hidden reason why he or she doesn't want to chase the $300,000 limit. Another thing: if I keep showing homes in the wrong

price range and the wrong neighborhood, what's Tom going to think about me? Maybe that I'm incompetent. Or pushy. Or that I'm not on his same wavelength. Then I might lose him as a client. So let your purchasers buy what *they* want to buy.

Question: Suppose there aren't any All-American homes available for Tom to purchase?

Answer: Hey, today's my lucky day! Now I can call up my title agent and ask for the addresses in a particular community along with the telephone numbers. Then I can mail a postcard to All-American homeowners, and follow up on the mailing with phone calls. "Hi, my name is Bob and I was wondering if you got my postcard. Are you thinking about making a move in the next six months or so?"

I get to be proactive and help Tom find the perfect house in the neighborhood he wants. Isn't it exciting? I have a purpose to canvas the neighborhood to look for listings. In fact, I might even say to myself, "Working with buyers isn't for me. I'm going to become a listing agent!"

That's no problem. But don't just sit there and talk about it. Do it!

In "Why I Wrote This Book," I told you about my buyer in the wheelchair. That two-timing, hotshot listing agent got me so angry that I doorknocked and telephone-canvassed the entire neighborhood until one day I found the perfect home for my friend. The woman who owned the home said that her mother had recently passed away. I showed it to my buyer who fell in love with the home and the seller fell in love with my buyer's eleven-year-old daughter. See, the seller had felt lonely after her mother's passing away, and having the little girl walking about the house cheered her up.

Guess what? A seller who was going to list the home with her best friend listed with me. And because I'd brought both the buyer and seller together, I made twice the money I would have made on the other house. To be honest, to me it was never really about the money. It was about conquering a meanness of spirit and in the end, things really did work out for the best. Don't you agree?

Question: What if Tom doesn't like any home I show him?

Answer: Remember, one of my first goals is to determine Tom's neighborhood. What happens with many new agents is that John is prequalified to $300,000 and because he's single they assume that Tom is a Yuppie. They only show him places from $280,000 - $320,000. But Tom could also be a Sexy Single, couldn't he? Or an Eclectic or an All-American?

> "Nothing's impossible if you want it bad enough."
> — Ben Hogan
>
> "You miss 100% of the shots you
> never take."— Wayne Gretzky

So make sure that you show three neighborhoods first. Let Tom tell you what neighborhood he likes in order to get a better idea of what kind of bird it is you're dealing with, even if Tom doesn't like any home he sees initially.

TIPS ON SHOWING HOMES

Here's a mistake I used to make when I first started selling real estate. After showing a home, I would say to a buyer: "Well Joe, did you like that home? How would Joe usually answer that question?

Joe is a bird.

The odds are that Joe would answer it by saying either "Yes" or "No" and either way I don't think that those are very informative answers.

Then I made a surprisingly simple realization. Joe is a bird. Birds will answer yes or no all day long if you let them. So, don't let them. It's a defensive posture. Kind of like when you go into a department store and the salesperson says: "Need any help?" Your answer is almost always the same: "No, thank you. I'm just looking."

Right? "Just looking" is a defensive tactic. It means, "No, I don't want to be bothered." John's "no" answer is also defensive. He may not feel like talking.

What should you say to make him come out of his defensive shell?

Bob's Insider Advice: The next time you want to say the word "like," bite your tongue and use the word "feel" instead. Let me repeat: use the word "feel" instead of "like."Why? Because homes are sold on emotions, aren't they?

Let's put it to work and watch what happens to Joe.

Bob: "How did you **feel** about that last home, Joe?"

Joe: "What do you mean, 'How do I feel?'"

Bob: "You know, your feelings? Your impressions? Was the kitchen spacious enough for you, John? Did you feel comfortable with the neighborhood?"

Now I pause and let him answer. Joe: "Oh, I get it. The kitchen was alright, I guess. The neighbors seemed to take care of their yards. I don't know. It wasn't too bad."

Do you see how Joe is forced to show the cards in his hand? Indirectly he's telling me that the yard, kitchen and neighborhood met his requirements. I'm getting closer to showing him what he wants. Do you see how Joe opens up for me when I asked him about his feelings? When you get birds to express themselves, you'll make more sales!

FAIR HOUSING ONE MORE TIME

If a bird comes into your office who is Hispanic, do you only take him to "Hispanic neighborhoods"? No. Or if the family is Black, do you only take them to "Black neighborhoods"? The answer is no. That's violating fair housing laws.

I had clients from Peru who barely spoke English but they refused to live in a neighborhood filled with Hispanics. "This neighborhood is all Hispanic, Bob," they told me. "We're Hispanic but we don't want to live next to other Spanish-speaking people. That's why we're moving!"

A word of advice about profiling buyers. Do not take too seriously what anybody tells you about certain buyers (and that includes me). Things aren't always the way they seem to be, remember?

Don't take it for granted that because the client is African American or Mexican American that they might want to live in a Black-only or Hispanic-only neighborhood. Let the clients pick the neighborhood and keep in mind that every buyer is an individual, different in many ways from every other buyer living, different even from his or her own identical twin!

Also be careful with your advertising. The Oregon Newspaper Publishers Association bans "bachelor pad," "executive" and "exclusive" from their ads. Why? They might seem innocuous to you but they may be construed as being discriminatory to a minority. Phrases like "near jogging track" is said to warn off the disabled; "close to church and synagogue" can offend atheists. The situation may seem ridiculous to you, but it's a serious situation. Your well-intended ad may be unintentionally offensive to a minority, so please check with your broker and follow his or her guidelines for advertising.

EXPERT BIRD-HANDLING PHRASES

Another part of our job description as agents is to smooth buyers' ruffled feathers.

I've seen buyers get so frustrated with the entire nerve-wracking process that he or she started shouting at a spouse! Squawking in front of me (as if I were invisible), ranting, raving and arguing over something minor. Or a buyer might fly off in a huff and pout because he or she couldn't find a special feature. Has this kind of thing ever happened to you?

Well, eventually it happens to all real estate agents.

There are many buyers who act like fussy, temperamental birds. So we buyer's agents have to be expert bird handlers.

Here are some phrases that may make handling your birds a little easier.

"No problem" I think it's a mistake to argue with buyers. Instead of objecting, use this phrase. "No problem." Death and taxes might be a problem, but everything else is just a challenge.

"Pop on in" This phrase is good to use to pick up necessary paperwork and to allay the buyer's fears about taking another step in the home buying process. These words also make it seem like the effort is no trouble at all to you. "Susan, it will take me only a minute to pop on in." Or "I'll be in your neighborhood this afternoon around 5:00. I can pop on in if you'd like."

"In addition to that, is there anything else?" This phrase is good if the purchaser seems bothered by something but won't open up and tell you. Pause after you say it. Frank Bettger is credited for it in his book *How I Raised Myself from Failure to Success in Selling.*

"Got it." This phrase will stop a long-winded bird in his or her tracks. Use it sparingly to cut off negativity about a home or neighborhood.

"I kinda got a feeling" or "I kinda get a vibe." Use these phrases to start the conversation rolling about something obvious that you noticed. "I kinda get a vibe that you liked that garage, Charlie."

"By the way..." An excellent phrase that helps bring pen to paper. Sam and Kim are raving about the swimming pool. After agreeing with them, you add, "By the way, Sam, did you want me to include the pool equipment in the purchase price?"

"Let me make a note of that." This phrase is a favorite of Tom Hopkins. Whenever a client shows interest, make a note of it. (Hopefully you'll be writing some of these notes down on a purchase agreement!)

"Let's put it in writing" or "Can I get that in writing?" These phrases should become a part of your working vocabulary as a real estate agent. One time, for example, a home inspection revealed asbestos in the airducts and the purchaser wanted the removal work to be done by a licensed contractor. The listing agent told my agent that the work had been done as requested. When she told me that the work had been completed, I told her, "Great, get it in writing."

Knowing that the purchaser had requested the work to be done by a licensed contractor, she asked the man on the phone, "By the way, can you put something in writing to prove that you are licensed to do this kind of work?" Guess what? He couldn't do it and the seller ended up having to hire another contractor to do the job. Things aren't always what they seem to be, right?

I'M A NICE CLIENT, BUT I WON'T
TELL MY FRIENDS TO BUY HERE

I'm a nice homebuyer, you all know me. I'm the one who never complains, no matter what kind of service I get. I'll sit at your desk and wait while you chat with another salesperson instead of with me. I just wait because I'm a nice client. It's the same when I go to a store to buy something. I don't throw my weight around. I try to be thoughtful of the other person. If I'm served by a bored salesperson who gets perturbed when I ask to see several things before I make my choice, I'm as polite as can be. I don't believe in rudeness.

Recently, after I bought a home, I found that the garbage disposal was defective. I hated to call my agent, but I thought she would know what to do. All I wanted her to do was to come over to the house and look at it. But I never got the chance to tell her because she was too busy telling me that it was now my problem. She said that it was my fault for not buying a home warranty. So, I just smiled and said "good-bye."

I never complain. I never criticize. And I wouldn't dream of making a scene as some people do. I'm a great client... and I'll tell you something else. I'm the kind of guy who will never buy from you again, nor will I recommend you to any of my friends and relatives. That's my little revenge for getting pushed around. That's why I take whatever you hand out...because I know I'm never coming back. I don't relieve my feelings by telling you what I think of you. My revenge is much more deadly than that.

In fact, a nice client like me, multiplied by others of my kind, can just about ruin a business. And there are a lot of nice people like me in the world, with lots of friends and relatives too. When you've been pushed enough, we go down the street where they're smart enough to know that clients like me are their number one priority. I'm a nice client but you won't see me here again.

CHAPTER THIRTEEN
The Seven Deadly Sins

Have you ever purchased something that required you to assemble it? Book shelves, a barbecue or a child's toy? I bet if you'd never assembled one before and weren't good at following directions, you might make a few mistakes, right? And after successfully assembling it once, you'd probably tell a friend, "Listen, if I were you, I'd buy this thing pre-assembled!" Or you might say, "Listen, if you need any help putting it together, call me, because I've made every mistake possible. I'll give you some pointers of what **not** to do." That's the way I feel about this particular chapter because I've made my share of mistakes in working with real estate clients.

In this chapter we're going to review mistakes that many buyers' agents make. Now, everybody makes mistakes so don't feel bad if you're guilty of making one too. What I want to do is discuss how to overcome these errors to make you surprisingly better.

I'll tell you
what **not** to do!

Sin #1: Wait For Buyers To Come To You; Don't Prospect For Them.

Prospecting is like dieting in reverse. Most people *hate* to diet, but they do it because they want to lose weight, right? Losing weight will make them feel better. But does a dieter lose twenty pounds overnight? No, proper dieting takes time and discipline. Likewise, most agents hate to prospect, but they do it because they want to make money. They know that prospecting will make their wallet fatter. Does that happen overnight? No it takes time and discipline. But just like dieting, it's easy to get off track. The first donut you eat often kills your diet, right? Likewise, the first day you *don't* prospect can lead to a month of not looking for potential buyers or sellers, right? (Say yes.)

Recently I went golfing with a friend whose mother has been in real estate for 25 years. She's very successful. Her house payment is $6,500 per month. When I asked him the secret to her success, he answered, "prospecting". He said, "Every day in between appointments, my mother is on the phone, making cold-calls or sending out mail." Imagine that. Twenty-five years in real estate and she is still prospecting!

Boy did that make me feel guilty. Here I was playing golf with her son!

My point is, if you believe that buyers magically come to top agents without these top agents doing something to attract them, you're committing deadly sin number one. You've got to constantly go out and beat the bushes in the

I'm pounding the pavement!

real estate business.

Many agents who work only with buyers are not fond of prospecting. They'll say, "Prospecting is not my thing. I'm Susan Smith's buyers' assistant. I only show homes." Or "The reason I became a buyers' agent is because I don't like to prospect."

Some words of advice on this issue. The key to having a bad month is to avoid contacting people. You can also play video games on the Internet, watch soap operas, hang out in bars and go shopping in your free time. All those things will help your career slide too.

Whether you're a listing agent or a selling agent, if you're a smart real estate agent, you'll prospect constantly, even with people who have already purchased

a home from you in the past.

As Roger Butcher says: "You've got to make contacts in order to make contracts."

If you don't have a database, get one. Then start using it.

Now, if you're new and/or part-time and need a good prospecting piece, copy the postcard found on page 133, fill it out, and mail it to some apartments. It works!

Sin #2: Assuming Too Much.

If I want buyers to react positively to me, I can't assume that a buyer is going to purchase a home from me just because I'm a nice person. I've got to give people something of value. Information on monthly payments, comparable sales data or even a scratch pad with the phrase, **Notary Public or Free Area Maps** on it (along with my contact number and address) are all good things people can use.

What **not** to do is to assume too much.

Ever notice that when you assume something and don't check out information, things have a nasty habit of not working out? It's true. If I assume that a home is available and show it without checking on this, the house has often already been sold. If I make an assumption about what kind of homes my client wants without first asking, I'm usually wrong. If I assume that the interest rate is going to be the same as it was last Friday, it's probably changed.

I once read a letter in the Dear Abby column about a woman who was taking a ferry to Vancouver. She got out of her car, sat down on a bench, and watched as a man approached and sat down next to her. Then she was shocked when he picked up "her" candy bar, ate it, put "her" newspaper under his arm, and walked away! Upset, the woman followed him to the dining area where he sat down to read the paper. He was holding a sandwich in one hand and the paper in the other. She walked over, grabbed the sandwich, took a bite from it, and gave it back to him. Satisfied, she went back to her car to retrieve her umbrella. There, much to her surprise, *she found her newspaper and candy bar.* They'd been there all along!

Don't assume too much. It's an easy way to make an embarrassing mistake.

Sin #3: Telling Too Much/Not Asking Questions or Listening

People told Linda, "You love to talk. You should get into real estate." But when Linda became a buyer's agent, she talked herself out of five sales before she learned that smart agents *ask questions* and let their clients do the talking. Then after the client chats, they nicely ask for the order. Now sometimes you don't have to say *anything*. You can just stay silent and use the silence to your advantage. See, the trick to being a bore is to talk only about yourself, your spouse and your children. Another way to be irritating is to top every story your buyer tells you with a better one that you know. Ever do that? Don't.

The second half of Sin #3 is *not listening to the client after you ask him a question.* Some agents will ask a question, but then won't hear the reply because they are too busy thinking of something to say next.

Pay attention to your client when he or she is talking to you, and don't try to overhear the conversation at the next table, or the football game in the background.

Try to do 50% less talking and 50% more listening.

Ditto for when clients ask for your opinion on how to handle a problem. Let's say a client says, "Bob, I like this home but it's got these hideous curtains. You've been in real estate for a long time. What do you recommend?"

Now I could spend ten minutes spewing pearls of wisdom, but I've found the following response to be effective. "Gee Tim, I don't know. What are you thinking of doing?" Then I'll just sit back and listen. Usually people have lots of good ideas and they're eager to tell me them. So I let them sound off. Afterwards, I'll give them a word of praise. "Oh, I see, you're going to put vertical blinds in the living room. Got it. Good, I like that idea."

Tom Hopkins has a great quote that you might want to keep in mind: **"When I make a statement of fact, people doubt me. When I ask a question, and when answering they make the statement of fact, people believe me."**

Sin #4: Just Showing Up/Not Knowing How To Work.

Many new people and part-time agents flounder because they just show up. This is different from not knowing what to do. These agents have not learned that there is a difference between doing just enough to get by and doing a first-rate job when you're in the office. They just show up and do crossword puzzles or play solitaire on the computer.

What makes a good worker? Punctuality, company loyalty, pride in performance, and productivity are all key ingredients. But top agents are self-reliant. They are available on Sundays to show property. They are organized and can call a purchaser from home without calling the office. They spend time prospecting when not in the office. They do personal errands on their days off. They go the extra mile and they reap the rewards.

Great agents even tell the world that *they like their work.* Their feelings about work shape their clients' feelings too. If showing homes is a chore to you and you show it, your clients will get the message. If you enjoy your work, be sure to let the enjoyment show.

What not to do is give up or even get angry when a buyer says, "There's something about this home that I don't like." Even though you may find the situation to be frustrating, listen to the client. Because isn't it true that **a buyer who seems to like everything never buys anything?** I think so! Don't give up if a buyer seems concerned about something. Romance them a little more. Romance them even

There's something I
don't like

when the home is in escrow. Sell them on the benefits again even if you have to show the home to their Uncle Harry who hasn't liked anything since the Johnson administration.

Give a big smile to your clients too. An agent who constantly complains is going to be as popular as a monthly bill. Try this technique. The next time somebody asks you a stupid question and you want to shake them by their shirt collar, send out some positive vibes. Repeat this saying over and over in your head. Make it your mantra: **"I wish you happiness, I wish you happiness, I wish you happiness."**

Sin #5: Calling a Duck A Horse.

In real estate, many of us kid ourselves. We say that we're going to make eight sales this month. That's our goal, eight sales by Tuesday, September 30th. Next, we write a To Do list every morning. But then many of us don't achieve our goals. We make one sale and we act like we made eight. We think we're a champion thoroughbred even though we're more like a duck! Are we being completely honest with ourselves? No.

It's tough to keep achieving sales goals. That's why it's important to post them on your bathroom mirror and keep written tabs of what you're doing in order to achieve them.

What not to do is to not keep records of your efforts.

Here's what I mean. If you were a compulsive spender and you went to a therapist for help, what would a therapist have you do? Most likely, he or she would have you keep track of your expenses. Every day you would write down where you spent your money. Why? You need to know how you're spending your money in order to spend less.

Now in real estate, many salespeople are compulsive **time spenders**. We come into the office at 10:00 a.m. and spend an hour on the phone. Then we preview two new listings and go to lunch. After lunch, we write five thank-you notes, meet a home inspector for our one sale this month, and then go home and pick up the children at 3:00 p.m.

Is that a very productive day? No. But we commit Sin#5 when we tell ourselves that it was. Let's suppose that we created a list of what we did that day. We'll call it our "Right Things I Did" list. On it, we'll write down the things we did right for that day.

Right Things I Did

T.M. (Things you did right for This Month)	N.M. (Things you did right for **Next Month**)
1) Previewed two new listings for client. 2) Met home inspector.	1) Sent five thank-you notes.

Let's see, you did write five thank-you notes, met a home inspector, and previewed two listings. That's good, but you can do better, can't you?

Maybe tomorrow you could pass out twenty flyers to the neighbors of those two new listings. You could visit two past clients and spend ten minutes with each of them. You could see a lawyer or accountant and ask him or her to send you some referrals.

Passing out flyers and visiting a lawyer's office isn't always fun, is it? No. Yet afterwards, you feel great. You did something you didn't like to do. Something unpleasant.

I think in the real estate business you need to be honest with yourself. We all pump ourselves up with positive thinking and sometimes we delude ourselves. You need to do things that will bring money for next month and usually **those** things are not much fun. In addition, you don't get credit for doing stuff you don't like to do. One time I showed homes for three hours in 110-degree heat, and I came home exhausted that night. When I told my wife what I did, and she looked me straight in the eyes and said, "Big deal. You're supposed to show homes. That's your job, isn't it?"

One night I did a brilliant job of getting a price accepted so the next day I mentioned it to all the people in my office. "Guess what?" I announced. "I got a seller on Ermine Street to accept ten thousand less than asking price. Man, was it tough. That seller didn't want to go down a penny." One agent rolled his eyes, and somebody else said: "Whoop-de-doo!"

Whoop-de-doo!

Why? Because real estate agents are **supposed** to do these things. You're supposed to show homes in hot weather and get sellers to approve our buyer's purchase agreements, right? So who gives you a pat on the back when you actually do them? **Nobody.** That's the beauty of the "Right Things I Did" list. You give yourself a pat on the back for doing things you really don't like to do. And when you get a pat on the back, it encourages you to go out and do more stuff that you probably don't really like to do.

It's like a football coach who gives praise to his players instead of yelling at every little mistake. I once was showing homes to an assistant football coach who was on the coaching staff of a high school football team that had won something like thirty-six games in a row without a defeat. I remember attending one of the practices and watching as the fullback ran through the middle, and then got tackled by the middle linebacker and fumbled the football. Tweet, tweet, tweet went the whistle. The head coach, his face beet red, ran to the pile.

I shook my head as the coach approached the two players. When I played football, our coach would have the whole team run whistle sprints whenever a player fumbled. Instead this coach grabbed the middle-linebacker, the player who had caused the fumble, and lifted him up by the face mask. He then screamed into his face: "That was a great tackle, Tony! Way to hit him, man! Way to go!"

Next, the coach walked over to the fullback and placed his arm on his shoulder and said something loud enough for everybody to hear. "Come on Jimmy, you can do better! Churn those legs and don't let anybody get that ball from you. Now, let's do it again."

The fullback trotted back to the huddle with both fists clenched, eager to show the head coach that he could do better. And the middle linebacker didn't walk back to the huddle. I think he floated. Is it any wonder why these high school kids won game after game, year after year?

Again, how do you do it? I suggest that you keep a ledger and objectify your performance. Every day jot down the "Right Things I Did Today" on them. Lard your ledger with daily accomplishments. It will spur you to succeed and gradually you'll begin to curb your duck desires.

Even if you just transferred 5 new contacts to your database, write that down. See if this idea helps you become a champion thoroughbred instead of a duck.

SIN #6: GETTING TOO PERSONALLY INVOLVED

The next sin that some agents commit is getting too personally involved with one particular client to the exclusion of everyone else. It's important to be genuinely committed to providing excellent customer service but some agents will spend 99% of their time working to make a miracle happen for one person, and then at the end of the month have nothing to show for their effort. Then the "friend" says, "thanks for your help but I don't think that we're going to buy after all. I guess it wasn't meant to be."

It's one thing to try and help qualified, motivated buyers with good credit, and another thing to be spending time on somebody who may need a miracle to help them get what they want. Miracles do happen, but I think that sometimes some of us need to say, "no" more often. Or "Sandy, I have a **deadline** I'm working on, so I can only spend about five minutes with you today." Most people will give you breathing room when you have to meet a deadline, ever notice that? Deadlines are important, aren't they?

Question: What's the deadline you're working on?

Sorry,
I have a deadline!

Answer: Achieving your goals by month's end!

Because there are a lot of buyers in the world who aren't picky or who **don't** have hard luck who also desperately need to buy homes. Why not schedule some time to look for these people? Have empathy for clients, nurture a human bond with them, help them, educate them and do favors for them. But try not to get too personally involved.

SIN #7 ALLOWING ANGER TO HURT OTHERS

If you're a person who is prone to getting angry, or you want to learn how to better deal with anger, you may want to purchase a copy of a book called *When Anger Hurts, Quieting the Storm Within* by Mathew McKay. One of the issues that I found interesting when reading it, is that many people think that venting anger or "blowing off steam" is psychologically healthy. **Instead, studies have proven that venting anger actually makes things worse!** Blowing off steam breeds fear and resentment! It causes stress, heart attacks and ulcers and makes Mr. or Ms. "hair-trigger-temper" feel even angrier the next time something happens!

So if you're a salesperson who loves to rip into an escrow officer when something goes wrong, or scream at a loan agent, fellow Realtor ®, buyer, seller, wife, husband, son, daughter or significant other when you get angry, STOP DOING IT. Please learn to control your temper. The book that I've mentioned above may save your life.

Run with me on this one...

If you're a person who has **never** lost a sale, hang in there, friend. You will. Or if your face never turned red with embarrassment because you showed a property and wrote a contract on it because you were told that it was available, only to discover that the house was already sold, take a number and stand in line. This kind of thing happens to everybody. So quit moaning about it. Learn from your mistake. Perhaps next time you'll talk directly to the listing agent to see if it's available, instead of relying on the office receptionist. The thing not to do is to yell at somebody.

I know what it's like. Sometimes you feel like screaming at a client, a lender, an affiliate, a fellow agent, etc., but don't. Bite your tongue and count to ten if you have to. Pull weeds, exercise, or find something constructive to do. Jog for ten minutes in your back office, but blowing off steam doesn't

help anybody.

Now to be fair, we've all made our share of blunders, too.

There is one agent in my town who went on a walk-through inspection with the client two days before the house was to close escrow, and the client said: "This isn't the house we made the offer on. We wanted the house with the fire-place."

So keep in mind: it's not the problem, but *how you react to a problem* that separates the great agents from the rest of the pack.

If you have a major challenge, something that might ruin your transaction, you owe it to your clients to call them up immediately. If you told a buyer that they only needed $6,000 to close escrow and Craig the lender says it's really going to be $9,000, don't wait till the last minute to tell them. Be aggressive. Do it now.

If you feel like exploding over something that's gone wrong, keep your voice level and try to talk out your feelings. "Craig, let's not get defensive and point fingers. I'm asking for your help here. I told the buyer they needed $6,000. How can we work this out?"

Bob's Insider Advice: Remember, it's not what happens to you, but how you react to what's happened to you that counts.

IMPORTANT NOTICE

Are you or any of your friends or relatives interested in owning a home in this neighborhood? You can now purchase a home for just 3% total down payment!

Street name: <u>Stillmore</u> Bedrooms: <u>3</u> Baths: <u>2</u>

Approximately <u>$3,750</u> total cost to move in.

The asking price is: <u>$125,000</u>

Qualifications:

1) **Owner occupant:** Buyer must be owner-occupant to qualify for this low down pmt.

2) **Credit: Decent credit.** Bankruptcies are allowed as long as discharged 2 years ago.

3) **Income:** Enough verifiable income to pay mortgage. Two years taxes required.

4) **Deposit:** A good faith deposit of $2,000 will go toward down payment and closing costs; any refund will be provided at close of escrow.

Please call me immediately for details.

Bob Boog

Office: (805) 555-1212

Pager: (805) 555-1221

This mailing piece works well on red paper. Why? Because many apartment tenants race to read it fearing that it is a rent increase, or something important. Try it in Red!

CHAPTER FOURTEEN
The Hot Buyer Club

Many real estate agents have their clients sign a buyer-broker agreement. This agreement spells out all the duties and responsibilities of the agent and allows an agent to collect a fee in the event the purchaser buys a home through somebody else. In some states having a written contract with a buyer is a requirement, and while many agents use one, I don't. If you currently use one, and enjoy success with it, terrific. Keep up the good work!

In California, where I live, the state association of Realtors® offers a comprehensive four-page buyer-broker agreement that covers details from A-Z. Some agents don't have a problem explaining the **agent's compensation.** I did. I found that many buyers suddenly turned nervous while others got cold feet. It's not quite as dicey as having your fiancée sign a pre-nuptial agreement, but it's pretty close. For this reason, I created my own form.

My one-page agreement is surprisingly buyer friendly and easy to use. It's called The Hot Buyer Club. When a purchaser agrees to join my club, he or she agrees to get preapproved with a lender and work exclusively with me for a period of three months. In return for their loyalty, I'll agree to provide them with a home warranty (worth $300) and a coupon for the first service call (worth $35) payable at the close of escrow. In the event that the buyer purchases a home **through another agent**, within the three months of our agreement, **the buyer agrees to pay me three hundred and thirty-five dollars ($335).** That's really all there is to it.

You might feel that $335 is not enough money, or that three months isn't long enough. Or that this form doesn't cover certain legal issues. No problem. Check with your broker first to see what amount is acceptable, or if this idea can be used in your area at all.

The reason I have buyers sign a registration form is to avoid the "Al and Evelyn" syndrome. Al and Evelyn were a friendly elderly couple who said they wanted to buy a home from me. I met them on a Saturday when I happened to be very busy. I neglected to have them join my hot buyer club and sign the registration form. Normally I'll have a client approve it at the same time they sign a credit authorization form. In this case, I had another client on the phone, my assistant was out and as I watched Al and Evelyn fill out the credit authorization form, I thought of the perfect home for them.

You can probably guess what happened. They later bought the bitchin' home I showed them through somebody else.

Why did this happen?

I could make all sorts of excuses but the bottom line is that I was harried so I took a short cut. I didn't fax their credit authorization form to my lender and wait for his call back. Instead we left the office in a hurry, saw two homes and when we got back to the office, another client was waiting for me. Evelyn told me: "Bob, you're busy. We'll call you."

I tried to call them that evening, but apparently they'd given me the wrong number. I kept getting the Wal-Mart pharmacy. True story. In fact, all the information on their credit authorization form was bogus. To top it all off, she even pocketed my favorite pen!

Let's review my mistakes so you can learn from my experience. Number one: I didn't fax the credit authorization to my lender. If I had done so, I might have learned that their mailing address or phone number was incorrect. Number two: I wasted time showing property to somebody who was a user. They probably had no intention of ever allowing me to be compensated. Right? They probably had a friend or relative in their hip pocket ready to collect the commission. Number three: They didn't join my hot buyer club. If they had signed my registration form, I might have earned either a commission or a check for $335.00. That's why it's important to go step by step with a client. So here are the steps to follow:

1) Have clients fill out a credit authorization form so that you get the basic name, address and phone number information.

2) Fax the information to your favorite lender or run the credit from your computer.

3) Then, while waiting for the credit to come back, explain that you offer a program to all your buyers whereby they get a home protection plan and service coupon. Most of them will want to join your club to take advantage of what you have to offer.

Who me?
Impersonate
a buyer?

This way, by having the correct names and signatures on a hot buyer club registration form, you can give them a list of homes and send them out to preview them on their own, without worrying about losing the clients to a competitor. Clients who don't qualify for a home may still refer your name to a friend.

You may still experience the Al and Evelyn syndrome, but by using the hot buyer club you'll be compensated for at least some of your time. And isn't that what we all want?

THE HOT BUYER CLUB
Registration Form

DATE: *11-22-98*

I, (We) ___*Denise Garcia*___ PURCHASER",
agree to buy a home exclusively with *Bob Boog* ,
hereby referred to as "AGENT". Agent will use due diligence to find a property for Purchaser. However purchaser agrees that in the event purchaser finds a home to purchase, with or without Agent's assistance during the next ninety (90) days from the above date, purchaser will work only with AGENT to fill out all contracts, disclosures and addendum's necessary to purchase said property. The consideration given to Agent today is $1.00

   In addition, PURCHASER agrees to cooperate fully with Agent and to promptly provide to Agent copies of the originals of the following financial items:
1) Last two-year's completed tax returns with W-2 and/or 1099 tax forms.
2) Three (3) recent paystubs to cover the last monthly pay period.
3) If self-employed, a year-to-date profit and loss statement.
4) Two recent bank statements or any banking information required by lender.
5) A credit report or signed credit authorization form to obtain a credit report
   In consideration of providing the above information, and working exclusively with Agent, AGENT agrees to provide the following to Purchaser:
1) A one-year home warranty at close of escrow. (A value of $300 dollars.)
2) A service coupon for one (1) free service call. (A value of $35.00 dollars.)
CANCELLATION FEE: In the event that Purchaser purchases a home without using the services of the above-mentioned Agent during the time period stated above, Agent will not provide home warranty or service coupon. In addition it is agreed that Purchaser will pay a cancellation fee to Agent in the amount of three hundred and thirty-five dollars ($335.00). Said fee will be paid within thirty (30) days of receipt of Agent's written demand, along with all costs of collection, if any. I also understand that all financial data given to agent will be kept confidential and destroyed if not used. I will not be given a copy of my credit report.

X	I HEREBY AGREE TO WORK EXCLUSIVELY WITH AGENT FOR 90 DAYS AND HOLD AGENT HARMLESS RE: MY FINANCIAL DATA.
	I HEREBY DECLINE TO WORK EXCLUSIVELY WITH AGENT FOR 90 DAYS AND AGREE TO PAY FOR MY OWN HOME WARRANTY.

Denise Garcia   *11-22-98*
_____
PURCHASER   DATE   PURCHASER   DATE
    Bob Boog   *11-22-98*
_____
AGENT   DATE

138

CHAPTER FIFTEEN
The Yin-Yang of Selling

This chapter covers a topic seldom discussed in real estate books, and originally I thought about not including it, but I decided the subject was important. Because the challenge in teaching people how to sell real estate is that the rules aren't always clear cut and you need to leave room for the agent to be flexible. Sometimes as a Realtor®, you do things a certain way for one client, and yet you might do things differently for the person's identical twin.

It's like the Chinese belief of Yin-Yang where a dual force affects people's lives. Sometimes it's hard to tell which force (the "feminine passive" or the "masculine active") has had a stronger effect in making a particular decision in your life. This happens in real estate. Though many times we think we know that a particular closing technique or question worked successfully, other times we're not altogether sure what caused the sale to be made.

I think that a key to remember in selling is to give people more than they expect to get. Do something extra for somebody.

Here's something that's embarrassing to me but true. For a short while, for some reason, I had a problem selling homes to African-American women. Each one was very picky and I had three experiences where nothing clicked. So when I met with another African-American woman client, I was determined to make the sale. Guess what happened? We wrote up four offers and got slammed on all four of them. Shiran finally told me, "Bob, don't waste your time. It's just not meant to be."

So I did two things. First I brought a video camera with me and I videotaped a home that I thought she would like. I figured that maybe she was just tired of getting in and out of the car. She really seemed interested in buying a home and had been prequalified, but she just didn't have time to waste. I needed to act quickly or I'd lose her.

The second thing I did was read a book about slavery. This may sound crazy, but it's true. Around the same time that I met this new buyer, I took a trip to the library to find a book for my son. While I was there I discovered the powerful work, *From Fugitive Slave to Free Man* by William Wells Brown. It's one of the best books I've ever read.

You see I didn't know if my sales experiences with these African-American women had something to do with me, that maybe I had missed something about these buyers. I thought maybe I could better understand something about these Black women, and my current client in particular.

During page one of this book, young William wakes up at 4:15 in the morning to the sounds of the overseer whipping a slave who was late to work. That slave happened to be William's mother. The whip was six feet long and made of cowhide and sharp metal.

Young William was powerless to do anything as he heard his mother scream while being whipped, and after I'd finished reading this compelling book, I remember thinking about it. Maybe my other buyers thought that I was as sensitive to their needs as the average schmoe. I felt that I had to prove to my new purchaser that I cared about her as a person.

Now I could brag and tell you that I sold a home to someone who simply watched a videotape in the comfort of her home and then insisted on making an offer, but I'm not altogether certain that I would be telling you the truth. Because I don't know if I would have taken the time to videotape the house if I hadn't read the book by William Wells Brown. Do you know what I'm saying?

I had a sincere desire to better understand another human's voice, and their way of looking at the world. That desire influenced my actions, didn't it?

The yin-yang of real estate selling is that sometimes we attribute a sale to one action which we feel directly contributed to the sale, but at the same time, there may have been another reason why the client purchased. Maybe it's a personal connection with the salesperson. *This salesperson cares about me. He or she did something extra for me.*

Nowadays there is a big push to buy into technology to make sales, but I think that many salespeople would be wise to also go low tech and simply care about their clients. Respect for another person's name, culture, religion and way of life can be far more effective than any arsenal of high-tech toys. One old-fashioned, handwritten thank-you note might make a more lasting impression than sending three efficient e-mail messages.

Invest time in understanding people better. I spent ten minutes one night practicing how to properly say one foreign client's name just so I wouldn't trip over my tongue and mispronounce it.

I've read up on Feng Shui for Asian clients, learned about Jewish holy days and Hanukkah. I've watched television programs in Spanish that Hispanic clients have recommended. In fact, Erik Estrada used to have a television show on the local Spanish channel called *Dos Mujeres y un Camino. (Two Women and One Road)*. It was a soap opera about a truck driver who was married and having an affair with a beautiful woman who lived on the other side of town. So whenever I showed homes to my Spanish-speaking clients, I would mention this program. Except that I would call it, "Dos Mujeres y un Cochino" (Two Women and One Male Pig). It never failed to make people laugh, and yet it told them I understood what was happening in the soap opera too, didn't it?

CREATE A "WHAT IF" MENTALITY

Finally, I think it helps to get in the habit of thinking "what if". When dealing with clients and challenges, constantly ask yourself, what if? What if I was this buyer? What if I was the seller? How would I look at this? What if we did things differently? By juggling a variety of concepts and solutions, you'll soon find yourself better able to solve challenges and avoid problems.

I guess what I'm saying is don't be afraid to take a risk, to make that extra effort, or to scribble outside the lines. It may be the very thing that helps you to win the sale. It may be the very thing that makes you surprisingly better than other agents too!

Each day before you begin work, devote 10 minutes to thinking, "How can I do a better job today? What special favor can I do for my customers? How can I increase my personal efficiency?"

— David J. Schwartz *The Magic of Thinking Big*

CHAPTER SIXTEEN
Answering Buyer Objections

Almost every book on selling real estate has a chapter on how to handle buyer objections, and my editor insisted that I write one too. I have to be honest with you. I dislike the term objection. The word objection reminds me of a courtroom where an attorney listening to a cross-examination of his client hollers out, "Objection, your honor!"

Buyers don't do this, do they? Can you imagine a buyer saying, "Objection Bob, the master bedroom is too small!"

Objection,
this bedroom
is too small.

Most buyers have **concerns**, not objections. Why? Because most people use their feelings as a guide in purchasing. So we have to listen to what the buyer is saying, formulate in our mind what it is he or she is really expressing, and then feed back the feelings he has expressed as you interpret them. The best way to do this is to feed back the feelings in the form of a question.

For example: Mrs. Lebec tells me, "Bob, I like this home but the bedrooms are too small."

"I understand how you feel, Mrs. Lebec, the bedrooms feel a little small?"

Now I pause and let her explain.

Oftentimes, after the pause, I'll get an answer like this: "Well, maybe this will be okay. My kids are sharing a room right now. I guess they don't need so much space if they each have their own room."

Oftentimes the problem that new people and part-time agents have, is that they believe they have to have a response for *every* concern that a buyer raises.

Not true! Now, sometimes there is a problem understanding what the buyer is saying. For example, Mrs. Buyer complains that she likes the home except that she can't stand the outdated carpeting, wallpaper and the house is on a hill. What the heck is she talking about?

If you don't understand what others are saying, ask them to clarify it for you.

"Let me see if I really understand what your concerns are. Please be honest and talk to me like a friend. Is it the carpet? Is it the paint? Is it the location of the house on the hill? Is it the money?"

See, sometimes the buyers themselves may not fully understand what they are trying to say.

Clarify her concerns by asking questions, and then listen closely. If living on a hill is a big deal, we may have to move on to another house. If she's only concerned about paint and carpet, try using the Feel, Felt Found technique.

"I understand how you **feel**, Mrs. Lebec. That carpet is hideous. Many clients **have felt** that all homes placed on the market should be in move-in condition. What we've **found**, however, is that sometimes we're able to negotiate a better price for a home that needs work. If you were to buy this home today, what do you feel you would offer for it?"

Again, listen to her response carefully. If she tells you that she doesn't want to live up on a hill, then honor her concern and move on to another home.

Bob's Insider Advice: Clarify concerns by asking questions. Feel, Felt, Found works great to ease a buyer's concerns.

Some buyers are complainers who are difficult to please. God love them. Others are like small children who constantly ask "why"? You answer one question and they'll come back with another question. One way to handle them is to answer their question with another question. The second way is to put the shoe on the other foot and ask "what if?"

Example: The buyer says: "Will the seller cut the grass for a year after they move out?"

Bob: **"What if** you were the seller and had sold the home, would you cut the grass for a year for your buyer?"

Now there are some buyers who will object because they simply need somebody to reassure them that they are doing the right thing. One time my son Kevin, age three, came toward his mother and myself. As he walked, tears rolled down his cheeks. He was holding out his little pointer finger and wailing so loud that I thought my next-door neighbors would call the police.

He must have cut his finger and we'll have to take him to the hospital and he'll need stitches. All of these thoughts flew through my mind. Then I noticed that as soon as his mother hugged him and kissed his finger, his tears evaporated, and a big smile crossed his face.

It was like the sun had evaporated all the clouds.

I say this because I once had a buyer named Blanca who called me after escrow was opened. She said she didn't want to buy the home anymore. She wanted to cancel the escrow and get her deposit back. I suppose I could have told Blanca that she had signed a binding legal contract, yada, yada, yada, but instead I suggested that we put down all her concerns in writing. She said, "Fine, I'll be at your office at 3:00."

When Blanca arrived at my office she brought her sister, so I suggested that the three of us look at the house one more time. That way Blanca could show her sister what was bothering her. When I opened up the house, I took out some comparable sales information to prove what a great opportunity this house represented but before I could say a word, Blanca marched into the kitchen holding a long piece of dental floss.

She didn't have a tape measure, and before I could go to my car to fetch one, I noticed a look of relief that crossed her face. "My fridge will fit," I overheard her say to her sister.

Blanca told me that she didn't think that her refrigerator would fit in the kitchen, but felt much better after seeing the home again. Guess what? She went ahead and closed escrow on the property. Now I don't know if she was really worried about the monthly payments or the refrigerator or the neighborhood, but the point is that Blanca had some concerns and wanted to be reassured that everything was going to be alright. She wanted to feel like she'd made the right decision.

No problem. Let me kiss your finger. Everything's going to be fine, isn't it?

CHAPTER SEVENTEEN
Product Knowledge

I want you to pretend for a minute that you're purchasing a parachute. If your life depends on the proper deployment of the parachute at a high altitude, would you purchase it from a brand new, part-time salesperson, or from an experienced parachute salesperson?

You'd probably want to purchase it from an expert, wouldn't you?

However you might not care if they were new or part-time at selling as long as they knew all about parachutes, right? And on the other hand, you wouldn't want to be sitting in an airplane on the morning of your jump and hear your salesperson say: "Boy do I feel nervous. Do you have a good life insurance policy? I hope so, 'cause I'm not sure if that chute I sold you is going to work."

Now where did that salesperson go?

That wouldn't make you feel very confident about jumping out of the airplane, would it? No.

Most home buyers also want to get a feeling of confidence from their salesperson. Many will be investing all their life savings, and they want you to prove to them that you know what you're doing. They want to feel secure. They also want to feel safe in the knowledge that you know how to figure monthly payments, how to negotiate contracts and how to calculate costs closely. If you don't know how to do these things, you need to practice, drill and rehearse them well enough that you could teach a class in it. You need to become an expert.

Bob's Insider Advice: all buyers secretly want a real estate agent to give them the feelings of confidence, security and safety.

Confidence, security and safety should become your mantra. The tricky part is to convey these feelings to buyers without being too obvious or talking too much. After all, how many people enjoy being lectured? Not many, right? **That's why it's so important to ask questions!**

Also, most buyers understand concepts better if you can relate examples to them. That's why I like the phrase, "what this means to you." Take, for instance, the concept of discount points. This is a subject that you have to explain to most buyers. Don't be afraid to use an example in which they can get involved: "Gary, let's pretend that you're a banker and I have two loans. One is at 7% interest and the other is at 8% interest. Which loan would you want to take?"

Note: Gary may give you the wrong answer here. He might say, "The loan for 7%."

Now I get to gently correct him. "Gary, remember, you're a greedy banker. Right? You want to make as much money as you possibly can. So which loan would appeal to you?"

Gary: "Oh, I get it. The one for 8% interest."

Bob: "Right. So what can I do to get you to take this loan for 7%? Suppose I gave you some money, two or three thousand dollars, that you could use to make a car loan at 14%, and you could turn this money over every three or four years. The amount of money I gave you, the banker, in order for you to give me a lower rate on the loan was determined by using discount points. Discount points are calculated as a percentage of the loan amount. What that means to you, is that if you want a slightly lower interest rate on the loan for the house you want to buy, it's possible for you to get it. It just costs more money."

Okay, maybe you have a better explanation of discount points. If so, use it. But keep in mind that the key is to give illustrations to clarify concepts in order to make them easier for a purchaser to comprehend.

What else?

A good buyer's agent has a sound working knowledge of homes. He or she knows, for example, that galvanized pipes tend to corrode more than copper pipes, and that if you see a plunger parked in the corner of the bathroom, there might be a plumbing problem with the toilet.

Here are a few more things to consider:

TAX RATES: A good buyer's agent finds out how much the taxes are, and if there are any special assessments, bonds or fees. How much would the taxes be if the property is purchased at your buyer's first asking price. An agent in New York, for example, told me that he sold a home for $45,000 and the taxes were $6,750 per year!

WHAT IS INCLUDED IN HOMEOWNER'S FEES? Most homeowner associations include trash collection, water, sewer, gardening, common maintenance and fire insurance in the monthly association fee. Some do not. A good buyer's agent will inquire of the officers in the association if he or she has a question. And if no officers can be reached, ask the owners in neighboring units.

HOW MUCH ARE LOCAL UTILITY BILLS? It is financially prudent for a purchaser to ask an agent or owner how much to expect to pay for normal utilities, especially if the purchaser is coming from out of state. Is the property using propane or natural gas? Some buyer's agents create a page that includes "average utility bills" in their resource book for buyers.

INSULATION: A thick layer of attic insulation is an energy saver. That's a no-brainer. In some areas, purchasers request the government rating on the insulation. Get it in writing from the seller, if possible.

WATER HEATERS: The Federal Housing Administration (FHA) requires that a pressure-relief valve drain into a pipe that empties into the ground, so look for a long copper tube – or galvanized tube that runs from the top of the water heater to the bottom. Also, in California, state law mandates that all water heaters be strapped for safety in the event of an earthquake.

THE COST TO RE-CARPET A HOME:

This question gets asked several times each year, so do yourself a favor and go to the carpet store near you and ask how much it would cost to carpet a 2,000 –square-foot home. Often the carpet salesperson will want you to physically measure the rooms. If this happens, you can ask for a simple formula for calculating this expense. Make a copy of it and keep it somewhere handy. (You'll be asked this question often, so be prepared!)

ROOFS: Visually examine the roof for missing shingles or ridge caps. Look for patched spots, areas of moisture and loosely attached gutters and downspouts. Inside the home, check to see if the ceiling leaks in obvious places, under bathrooms, and beneath roof-mounted air conditioners. If so, make a note of it in your purchase contract.

BASEMENTS: My father grew up in Minnesota and he used to say that a person could tell if a basement flooded by the amount of junk found in it. In other words, if an agent sees piles of stuff on the floor, it's likely that the house has a good basement. But if everything is up on stilts, raised six feet from the floor, it's likely the basement floods in the winter or spring.

EXTERIOR PAINT: Look for dried-up, crinkled facia boards. They are often called "the trim" and are located at the end of the roof. Why should you be concerned about them? FHA appraisers often require that exterior facia boards be properly sanded and repainted. Also look for rotten timber or signs of dry rot.

We're used to the basement taking in some water

SCHOOL DISTRICTS:

A good buyer's agent compiles a "Welcome to the Area" package that includes general information about the local schools and places of higher education. By providing a list of schools and phone numbers, buyers are encouraged to make their own inquiries.

DOLLAR-PER-SQUARE-FOOT- VALUE:

This subject requires more attention than some of the other points. Why is this topic so important? Dollar-Per-Square-Foot Value is a good, rule-of-thumb way to figure out if a property is competitively priced or it is over-priced

To calculate the dollar-per-square-foot price of a home, simply divide the selling price by the square footage. For example, if the house down the street sold for $140,000 and it spanned 1,400 square feet, the dollar-per-square-foot value would be $100 per square foot. ($140,000/1,400 = $100)

Question: A home in the Meadows tract is listed for $208,000 and is 1,955 square feet. What is the dollar-per-square-foot value?

Answer: $106. ($208,000/1,955 = $106)

Now let's use this value to compare this home to other homes that have recently sold in the same neighborhood.

1) 21601 Farmington — Sold for $165,000 and was 1,701 sq. ft. = $97 psqft

2) 28006 Newfield — Sold for $151,500 and was 1,530 sq. ft = $99 psqft

3) 28225 Stonington — Sold for $176,000 and was 1,814 sq. ft. = $97 psqft

The average dollar-per-square-foot value is $97.5

($97 + $99 + $97 = $293/ 3 = $97.5)

The dollar-per-square-foot value is a tool that helps buyers make an informed decision about what price to offer when there are no comparable sales **exactly** like the home you've shown your buyer. The buyer using this factor might feel that the value of the 1,955 square foot home in the Meadows tract might be closer to $190,000 than $208,000. ($97.5 x 1,955 = $190,612)

Sometimes a dollar-per-square foot value can be misleading. Smaller homes in a housing tract will often have a higher value than larger homes so you have to be careful not to misrepresent a property's value. There are other variables that may come in to play as well. For example, you might find that a home on **one** acre might **be worth more** than a home **on five** acres. Why? **Because many people don't want the upkeep of five acres.** And if the supply of one-acre homes is low and the demand is high, prices may be higher for one-acre homes, or vice-versa.

Talk to your broker or sales manager and ask if they use dollar-per- square-foot values when they compare homes. And some multiple listing associations no longer publish square footage values because of lawsuits. See what your broker recommends for your area.

Below you'll find a Comparison Sheet for buyers. I've taken this information and created notepads for buyers so that they can make notes about the homes they are considering.

New agents: Why not make up a page like the one on page 153 and take it with you on your next tour of homes? Pencil out what properties are listing for on a dollar-per-square- foot basis. When these homes finally sell, you'll have seen the interior condition of the property, and you'll be a better judge of value.

Comparing Houses

	Address	Address
Neighborhood	25211 Frost	26332 Roberts
Price	$242,850	$262,900
Sq. feet	1542	1431
Bedrooms	3	3
Baths	2	2

Rate the following features on a scale of 1 to 10. (Ten=best)

Appeal	8	7
Neighborhood	8	8
Heat/ac	Ch/fa	Ch/fa
Kitchen	Large	Small
Garage/extras	3 att	2 att

My rating for this house:

8.5	7.0
Sharp	Nice

I'll look up any home in any neighborhood for you!

_____

_____

_____

A DO'S & DON'TS LIST FOR BUYER'S AGENTS

DO: Keep a map, toilet paper, towel and a flashlight with fresh batteries in your car. Also a measuring tape, hammer, extra business cards, a legal pad and a calculator are good to have on hand as well.

DON'T: Leave the office without telling somebody where you're going and what time you expect to return. A serial killer could be lurking.

DO: Carry all necessary purchase contract forms/counteroffer forms. (You can store them in a briefcase you keep in your trunk.)

DON'T: Run out of gas, forget your lockbox key, or lock your purse in a house.

DO: Stay in shape. Walk, jog, lift weights, exercise. Sex sells!

DON'T: Act too sexy. People feel uncomfortable when an agent is on the make.

DO: Play your cards close to your vest.

DON'T: Tell your great ideas to title reps, loan reps or escrow people. It will spread like wildfire throughout the real estate community. (Likewise malicious gossip.)

DO: Write the price, terms and closing costs on a lined, yellow pad.

DON'T: Fill out the price, terms and closing costs on the purchase contract prematurely. Too many contracts are wasted because a buyer has changed his or her mind.

DO: Keep your promises.

DON'T: Call a horse a duck. If a client doesn't like a property for whatever reason, don't patronize the client by telling him or her that the property is something it's not.

DO: Encourage home inspections. Love at first sight is possible, but a second look is also advised.

DON'T: Be afraid to toot your own horn. Tell buyers that you need them to replace themselves with someone as nice as them! They will find somebody for you if you ask them!

CHAPTER EIGHTEEN
The Purchase Agreement Highlight Sheet

It's usually better to present a purchase contract to a seller in person, rather than faxing it to the listing agent, wouldn't you agree? An offer that's presented directly to the homeowner will seem more personal and therefore more persuasive.

It's also a good idea for the buyer's agent to convey to the owner what the buyer likes about the home. Many owners take pride in their properties and will favor someone who appreciates their home.

Sometimes you don't get a chance to do this. The seller lives out of town or the listing agent requests that all purchase contracts be faxed to him. But whether your purchase agreement is presented to the seller in person, or faxed to the listing agent, I've found that it's helpful to use a Purchase Agreement Highlight Sheet.

What is a Purchase Agreement Highlight Sheet? It's a form that when filled in by a selling agent, spells out the terms of the purchase agreement in easy to understand language. It helps to make a purchase agreement less complicated for both the seller and his listing agent. In addition, it tells the seller and listing agent a little bit about your purchaser and what your client likes about the home. Or what they don't like.

Sometimes one of the benefits is that it frees up your time. Let's say you've written a full-price offer and the market isn't blazing hot. You can drop off the offer with this form and say, "Mr. or Ms. Listing Agent, here is my client's purchase agreement. Please page me if you have any questions." Then you're out the door, and on to selling more houses!

Try using it sometime. It may come in handy!

Purchase Agreement Highlight Sheet

Property Address: _____

Buyer/Seller: _____

Offer Price: _____ Date of Offer: _____

General Information

1) What is the occupation of the purchaser(s): _____/_____

2) How long have they worked? _____

3) How much do they make per year? _____/_____

4) Have they been pre-qualified or pre-approved with a lender? Yes No

5) Name & phone number of lender: _____

6) How much is the deposit? _____ sonal check or Other

7) How much is the down payment? _____

8) Fixed rate or variable? (circle one)

9) Seller to pay points or closing c_____

10) Seller to pay for any repairs? Total: _____

11) Seller to carry a note? Yes N___ rms of note. _____% all due in _____ yrs.

Escrow/Title Information

1) Name of escrow compa_____ Phone( )_____ escrow officer: _____

2) Escrow time period: _____ D___ f scheduled close: _____

3) Name of title comp_____

4) Does contract say _____? Yes No

5) If Yes, who is the Nominee? _____

6) Any co-signor(s)? Yes N___ Was credit checked on them? Yes No

7) If so, names ___ co-signer_____

8) Is this a "short-sale___ No

9) Drop dead _____ort le approval: _____

Physical Inspection/Pest Control

1) Does contract call for a home inspection? Yes No
(If No, buyer to sign waiver addendum.)

2) When is home inspection scheduled to be done? Date: _____

3) Will the utilities be on for the inspection date? Yes No

4) When will the pest control inspection be done? _____

5) Name of pest control company: _____
   Phone( )_____

What we like about your home:

Our concerns: _____ s on:

Miscellaneous

1) Is house on sewer? Yes No (No, a septic certification will be required)
   Name of sewer/septic con _____

2) Is house on a water well? Yes
   (If yes, a well-certification will be required)
   Name of water well co _____

3) Is a survey required? Yes
   Scheduled date of survey _____ Contact: _____

4) Is an attorney inv _____ No
   If Yes, name of attorney _____ Phone( )_____

Home Warranty

1) Will there be _____ nt? Yes No

2) Name of warranty _____

3) Cost of home warranty _____ includes: _____

Homeowner Association No

1) Does property _____ to a homeowner association? Yes No

2) Month _____ ne fee: _____
   Fee inc _____

3) Is there any li _____ on against it? Yes No

4) Any special assessments? Yes No
   Amount: _____ Due: _____

5) Date the CC&R's are to be approved by buyer: _____

One Other Benefit

I've mentioned that the Purchase Agreement Highlight Sheet is useful to leave with the seller and the listing agent, but another benefit of using it is that sometimes you'll gather information about the property that you can pass along to your buyer, or save for future reference.

Here's an example of how I've used this sheet to inform my buyers. In my area after the 1994 Northridge earthquake, almost every condominium or townhouse in my area had a special assessment levied against it. These fees were different from one association to the next. In one condominium development, a buyer might have to pay the normal monthly association fee plus an extra $30 per month for an assessment, and in the next association, the normal monthly fee plus $15,000 payable in one lump sum. Some associations sued their builders, others didn't. Some developments required that all homeowners had to move out of their units for an entire year, others only had to have their garages retrofitted and didn't have to move out. It was a big mess.

Now as a buyer's agent, I wanted to know the most up-to-date information in order to better inform my purchasers. So I made it a point to fax a blank highlight sheet to a listing agent and I'd ask them to complete the homeowner association information. That way I'd have something in writing for my buyer to see before filling out a purchase agreement.

Make the Sunday Paper and/or Internet a Sales Tool

Along this same line, many sales have been made because the agent was prepared with information on the latest trends culled from the newspaper or Internet. Are mortgage rates heading downward? That might mean that purchasers should buy before the prices go up. Is the bond market nose-diving? That might indicate that mortgage rates may soon be rising. Clip out the article or download the information and save it in a special file. Then, instead of pressuring a client, allow them to read the news clipping while you "feel-felt-found" them. A news article or other information is extremely persuasive because it comes from an independent source. Try it and see!

For news about real estate related information, check out these web-sites:

www.cnn.com

www.niteowl.net

www.vahomes.org

www.fanniemae.com

www.latimes.com

www.bankrate.com

www.Realtor®.com

www.hud.org

www.freddiemac.com

www.eloan.com

www.quickenmortgage.com

www.homeshark.com

How to Maintain or Improve Your FICO Score

Question: What is a Fico Score?

Answer: Devised by Fair Isaac & Co. (based in San Rafael, California) the score, ranging from a low in the 300's to a high above 800 - represents a statistical evaluation of a borrower's risk of future default. A FICO score is produced by running a consumer's raw credit bureau data through computer software marketed by Fair Isaacs. The higher the score the better! Good credit is 620 or more. To maintain, or improve a score keep in mind these three rules:

1) Don't come close to "maxing" out your credit cards.

2) Pay everything on time.

3) Dispute any "derogatory" information in your credit history.

Remember there is no "quick fix" to repairing credit. The most rapid improvements in a credit score, however, can come when erroneous data sitting in your file is eliminated.

CHAPTER NINETEEN
Keep Your Attitude Up

The dictionary defines attitude as viewpoint, manner or posture. It's a way of looking at things. Somebody once said, "The most important factor in life isn't what happens to us, but the attitude we take toward what happens." We can't change the economy or what happened to us yesterday, but we can change our response to it. To become a surprisingly better agent, you've got to keep your attitude up.

Sometimes it seems easier said than done. For example, how do you keep your attitude up when your spouse or best friend has just died? How do you stay up when you feel sad? Or depressed? Or angry?

We real estate people are like soldiers. We march from house to house, sale to sale, and then we get up the next day and march again. Every day we have to be constantly on guard for dangers that lurk behind every corner. Problems with appraisals, termite reports, lenders, title companies, buyers and sellers. We have problems with our personal lives, problems with the competition, problems paying our bills. It's hard to keep a brave face and be courageous every day. So how do you keep your attitude up? Read on and I'll share some of my ideas with you.

Know Your Purpose

I think that you have to practice keeping your attitude up. How? Start by writing down the reasons why you sell. A mission statement will help you stay centered. Here's a sample mission statement. Yours may be different but it will give you a general idea: *"It is my mission to efficiently serve as many clients as possible. I pledge to act in a professional, ethical and responsible manner that safeguards my clients' interests as well as my own, because that is what my clients deserve and expect. In addition to negotiating contracts and finding the best value for my customers, I hereby promise to provide services for all my clients after their escrow has closed."*

Knowing your purpose makes you stronger and your job easier. Hold on to this objective dearly, for sometimes people want to take your job or reduce its importance. **Take the time now to create your own mission statement.**

Know Your Worth

There will occasionally be people who will say, "Why should we use you? We have the World Wide Web or Mary Smith, your competitor. Why should we use you as our real estate agent?"

To arm yourself against this type of negativity, write down three adjectives that you could immediately use to describe yourself. For example: I'm hard-working, and I'm enthusiastic, and I'm honest. Got it? Take out a sheet of paper and jot down three things you like about yourself like the examples below:

I'm ____joyful____

I'm _enthusiastic___

I'm __persistent___

When people think that you're worth more than the amount that they are paying, they have no problem paying it. But when they feel that they might not be getting their money's worth, then they won't want to work with you. Or they won't send you any referrals. They'll look to find some-body else. That's why we want to try to exceed their expec-tations and do just a little bit more for our clients.

Your success in selling homes, now and in the future, depends on whether you view yourself as being worthy of success. If you see yourself as being worthy of success and filled with abundance, other people will too. Question your worthiness and other people will too, and as a result your self-esteem and confidence will crumble.

A person filled with self-doubts conveys a feeling of uncertainty and buyers can sense this feeling. A house might be perfect for Brandon and Sarah but Nervous Nellie who is worried about making her car payment makes Brandon and Sarah feel uncertain about buying the home. Confident Carl has twice the problems as Nervous Nellie, but he makes Brandon and Sarah feel comfortable. Is it any wonder that this couple decides to purchase the same home that Nervous Nellie showed them with Carl and not Nellie?

Realize that many times buyers want us to help them make the right choices. That's why it's critical for us to be strong and ethical, to leave our self-doubts at home and let the client purchase the home that they want in the neighborhood that makes them feel comfortable. Always remember, it's up to you to remember your worth.

Remain Confident with a Little Help from the Poor Man's Computer

How do I keep my attitude upbeat if I'm having a sales slump? I'm glad you asked. I have what I call a "poor man's computer" to help me practice and keep my attitude up. Also, if you haven't mastered basic topics such as how to set goals, you might consider creating one. Now, what is a poor man's computer?

I'm going to tell you about it by sharing with you a series of events that occurred in my life.

I mentioned the Northridge earthquake earlier in the book. What I didn't tell you was my wife was nine months pregnant that morning and when the earthquake hit, I was afraid that she was going to go into labor. I was worried that I was going to have to deliver a baby on my front lawn with all my neighbors watching. Fortunately the baby waited; my wife gave birth ten days later in a hospital, thank God, on January 27, 1994.

But to this day I'll never forget that weird morning. For those of you who have never lived through an earthquake, here's what they don't tell you. Because when you see it on television, you say, "Okay, an earthquake happened. What's the big deal? Get over it, right? What you may not know is that there is one major jolt and then about ten thousand smaller aftershocks. And when a seismologist calls it an "aftershock," the word sounds like an "afterthought" or "after-dinner mint" but actually **it's another freaking earthquake!** It's a mini-earthquake. Not as strong as the initial one, but sometimes strong enough to shake a building so hard that block walls start wobbling and the whole house feels like it's going to fall down. (Believe me, it's not fun showing homes during an aftershock.)

Anyway, not one person on my street went back into their house during that first day because the aftershocks were still too strong. I wanted to be near a phone in case my wife went into labor, so I found an extra-long curly telephone cord and stretched it out from the connection in our kitchen to the front sidewalk where I was sitting. I wanted to know if my medical insurance would cover having a baby in a private hospital so I kept calling my insurance carrier every few minutes to find out, but the lines were always busy.

Then a funny thing happened, my phone rang. There I was, sitting out on the sidewalk, when somebody called me! I figured it must be my parents or my brother or some relative asking about my wife's condition, but it wasn't. It was the Internal Revenue Service. True story. The lady on the phone asked me about my 1984 tax return.

I couldn't believe it. I thought she was joking but she wasn't. I told her that an earthquake had just happened. She said, "I understand completely because I lived through the Loma Prieta earthquake here in San Francisco."

For those of you who have never had one of these computer snafus with the IRS, the way it works is every couple of years you get a letter from them. And in the letter you'll see that the past due amount has doubled or tripled. So you send them a letter and a copy of your cashier's check and you get a promise that it won't happen again. Then a few years later, it happens again. In my case, the original amount of $2,500 that I'd paid had turned into a bill of $34,000.

The lady from the IRS wanted a full payment of $34,000. I told her I didn't have it and that I could prove that it was a mistake but my garage looked like a tornado had hit it, and I had no idea where the copy of my ten-year-old cashier's check was. Besides, I reminded her, I had sent the IRS letters on this on several occasions and blah, blah, blah.

To make a long story short, I don't recall exactly what I told her, but whatever I said, it was not the right thing to say. Wrong, very wrong. Dumb. Very dumb. Because two days later when I went to a bank ATM machine and tried to get some money out, it wouldn't let me. My account had been frozen! Later I found out I was left with three hundred bucks.

Now I don't know if you've ever been broke, or about to have a new baby, or have ever tried to sell homes after a natural disaster, but let me tell you, if you combine all of these ingredients together at the same time, I promise you that you will not sleep well at night. I guarantee it.

I didn't know what to do. My wife said: "Go down to the Federal Emergency Management Agency (FEMA) and ask for some assistance. You'd better get us on welfare or something." Again, one of those events of my life I'm not too proud to admit, but it's true.

A few days after the earthquake, I went to the FEMA disaster center thinking I could get unemployment assistance. I stood in a line that went around the block and waited for about two hours and then I waited some more. And I waited inside this big tent for another two hours. Finally it was my turn. The FEMA director looked at my tax returns and reviewed my application.

"You own a business to sell real estate?" he asked. "Looks like you make good money."

"Yes sir," I answered. "But there was an earthquake and the IRS, blah, blah, blah."

He looked me in the eye and asked, "Do you still have a car?"

"Yes sir."

"Was it damaged by the earthquake?"

"No sir."

"Then you're still employed," he said. " Next in line."

Next!

Ouch! I realized soon after this conversation that I needed to figure out a way to become surprisingly better with buyers. I had to sell some homes, pronto.

I had a brand-new baby, a wife and a three-year-old son who were counting on me.

This is where some people say, "No problem. Just go out and get listings!" However, at the time, I did have some listings. Unfortunately, eight of them were located in condo associations and there was no way any of them would sell, not until insurance companies, etc could assess the damage. None of my sellers could put $15,000 into escrow to cover any future earthquake assessments. I had two homes listed that couldn't be sold in their present condition. I had the buyers of six escrows that were supposed to close the following week call me to say that they were canceling. Man, I didn't know what to do.

But I knew that if I could sell just one home, then I could sell another one after that and then another one after that. I thought to myself, I need to do something. But what should I do first?

Somebody had once told me, "Bob, a crisis situation helps to build character." Well, here was my opportunity to grow. Here's what I did.

I began by cleaning up my office. I figured there has got to be a silver lining in a situation like this. There has to be something good to keep me from being depressed. I knew it was there, I just had to find it.

Then I found it. The earthquake had miraculously transformed my $1,300 computer into a beautiful, new $1,300 paperweight! It's true. My computer had been changed into a heavy object that was only good for keeping papers from flying around the office when the wind blew!

Well, I needed a good paperweight because papers were scattered all over the floor. My office was a big mess. A water bottle had broken and many of the acoustic ceiling tiles had fallen.

Then Kimmy bounced in. Kimmy was an agent who lived outside the city and her home hadn't been affected at all by the earthquake. When she entered, she looked around and said: "Oh my gosh. What happened? Did we get robbed or something?"

I gave her the big news about the earthquake and she was so moved that she called her sister. Kimmy's sister also lived out of the area. She too hadn't been affected by the earthquake, and they were gabbing for a while and I couldn't help but overhear part of the conversation. Her sister had wanted to know the name of a pizza place that they'd visited five years ago. Kimmy remembered that she still had the phone number on her Rolodex®, so she went to her desk, found it, and rattled off the name and phone number. Then she hung up the phone.

Kimmy resumed helping me.

"What's going to happen with your Decoro Street buyers?" I asked Kimmy. "Do they still want to buy the place?"

"I'm not sure," she answered. "I misplaced their phone number at home, that's why I came here, to see if I could find their file, but it's missing. Their phone number is unlisted. I was going to get it off the computer, but now the computer is broken. What should I do?"

"Let's look for the file," I said. "It's got to be here somewhere."

That's when the idea of the poor man's computer dawned on me. It seemed ironic that Kimmy could find the phone number of a lousy pizza place for her sister, a restaurant that she hadn't been to in five years, yet she couldn't find the phone number of an important client who was about to close escrow! On a house that was going to bring money to her.

I got an idea. A brainstorm. Why not buy a Rolodex® and put all of my buyers and sellers in it and keep that Rolodex® on my desk? Because I couldn't afford to fix my computer, I invented what I call my "poor man's computer" or "people-moving computer." I called it my PMC for short.

To most people, my PMC looks just like a $5 Rolodex® that you can buy at Staples, but it's invaluable to me. I still have three of them on my desk. The first Rolodex® is for my hot buyers and sellers, the second one is for my past clients, and the third one is for general Rolodex® stuff, (escrow companies, lousy pizza places, mortgage lenders, attorneys, etc.).

Now you may or may not want to do this. You probably have a palmtop computer, a Dayplanner or a laptop with excellent client follow-up software that makes a Rolodex® as outdated as an Edsel. No problem. My hat is off to you. However, keep in mind the **yin-yang** aspect of selling in mind. A person who **only** uses high technology can be beaten by somebody like me who tapes his goals to the bathroom mirror. But somebody who only tapes his goals to a mirror can also be beaten by a salesperson with the latest computer hardware. Therefore I've found that it's helpful to use both: I tape my goals and I use a database.

Let me ask you a question though. What would you do if you couldn't use your computer? (And you couldn't afford to get it fixed or buy a new one.) What would you do? Let me tell you. Most likely, you would purchase a $5 Rolodex® and start filling it with the names of buyers and sellers, and anybody else who was even remotely interested in owning property. Then you'd give those people a call or you'd stop by their houses and see them.

You'd probably call on your past clients too. You'd write their phone numbers on the back of your hand if you thought it would help you remember to call them, wouldn't you? Sure.

Question: Why am I talking about this poor man's computer in a chapter about attitude? Because placed behind the phone numbers of all your hot buyers and sellers will be some motivational sayings and self-improvement reminders.

See, maybe your life has a kink in it. Perhaps something's happened to you in the past few months that has caused you to worry, and as a result, you're not as effective with buyers as you used to be. Maybe you're bouncing back from the death of a loved one. Maybe you're poor, or old, or you're ashamed of yourself or your family. Perhaps you're newly divorced or recently widowed. Maybe you have children with disabilities or your spouse is infertile, or maybe you are a mother who is just underappreciated. Whatever your problem might be, you could probably use a poor man's computer to help lift your spirits and give you a much needed shot of positive attitude.

That's what this poor man's computer is really about.

Every day you turn the cards on your "computer" and read some motivational sayings or self-improvement quotes. It's what I call "my daily dozen."

That's how a poor man's computer works: you program it with affirmations or inspiring words from people who have risen from defeat. You put those quotations on rotary cards and read them once or twice a day. I read mine before I meet with a client or go on a listing appointment.

Question: Do you feel that your present situation is tougher than Helen Keller's? How about Nelson Mandela's? Or Christopher Reeve's? Do you think Winston Churchill's advice might help you? (It was Churchill who said, "Never, never, never give up!")

Perhaps a better name would be PMAC (Positive Mental Attitude Computer)!

What I do know is that there is a proverb, "out of sight, out of mind." And I discovered that when times are tough, it helps to have everything in plain sight. The subconscious mind will direct you to read cards from that little Rolodex® every day if you program it. The Avery Company makes sheets of rotary cards that fit your laser printer too. Just like they make sheets of labels. Why don't you make up a PMAC? What will it cost you? Five bucks?

Question: What would happen if Tom Hopkins, Mike Ferry or Danielle Kennedy came to your office and personally gave you a short pep talk on prospecting tomorrow? Do you think you'd work harder? Sure you would. Do you think you might sell a few more houses? Maybe.

Some people say, "I've got his audio tapes. I'd play one of them."

Right. They're probably on a shelf somewhere gathering dust.

What might happen if you were in a sales slump five months from now and you wanted to tell somebody off? Suddenly, just like Kimmy looking for the pizza place, you absentmindedly flipped through the PMAC on your desk and you read something like "Smile big. People like you and trust you." Who knows? Reading that card at that time might save a sale for you.

I can't promise you that a poor man's computer will guarantee you one more transaction a year or save your escrows from falling out. But who knows? It might do something even more important for you! It might remind you to show some appreciation to your spouse. It might stop you from criticizing somebody close to you. It might even give you an unexpected boost when you needed it most.

Perhaps you don't care for Tom Hopkins, Mike Ferry or Danielle Kennedy. But you do like reading Zig Ziglar, Harvey MacKay, The Holy Bible and Og Mandino. Hey, no problem! The great thing about a poor man's computer is that it doesn't require a genius to program it. That's right dummy, you get to do it!

If you are new to real estate or in a sales slump, you might want to create a second computer and fill it with self-improvement stuff. Tom Hopkins, Mike Ferry, Rand Miller, Floyd Wickman and Brian Buffini all have excellent training programs. Why not plug into one of their programs and create a "training computer." Keep one at home and one at the office!

What's funny is that nobody notices it if you have two or three rolodexes on your desk. Nobody says: "That's against office policy. You are not allowed to have three rolodexes on one desk!"

Nobody will even care. And if they do, who cares what they think? That you're dumb? Hey, I've been called the dumbest agent in town and nobody's ever made a comment to me about it. Not even once!

As I mentioned, I was in a tight spot. The day we brought our newborn baby home, I got food and diapers from the Red Cross. I borrowed money from friends and relatives whose homes were also damaged in the quake. But I knew that if I could just keep my attitude up I'd get through all the sleepless nights. Like the little train that said: "I think I can, I think I can, I know I can, I know I can."

I even invented my own saying. I'll give it to you as a gift in appreciation for your taking the time to read this book. I hope you like the saying. But if you don't, that's okay too!

Frank Bettger, who wrote the classic book: *How I Raised Myself from Failure to Sucess in Selling* inspired me. He has the following saying: "*To become enthusiastic, I act enthusiastic.*"

It's a great precept. I use it all the time.

Here's mine: "**To become positive, I think positive thoughts. I can, I can, I can.**"

It doesn't matter to me whether you prefer my saying or Frank's saying, or maybe you like or dislike both of them. The point is to find what works for you.

Perhaps you are a fan of Denis Waitley, or Barb Schwarz, Dale Carnegie or Napoleon Hill. The idea is to keep their information fresh and in your face every day where you can see it. Not on the bookshelf gathering dust. If you said that your purpose reading this book is to close more escrows, then it's *critical* that you start flipping some cards. Try it for a week and see. It works.

Bob's Insider Advice: Why not create a training computer today? Make up twelve rotary cards apiece on these four topics: prospecting, goal setting, asking questions and enthusiasm. Then, every day for one week, read the cards. Give a week's strict attention to one topic. For the first week, for example, work on setting goals. Then the next week determine to

increase your prospecting, leaving the other topics to ordinary chance. Concentrate on the topic at hand. When you're finished with all four topics, start all over again! Four weeks is all it takes.

Now for those critics in the peanut gallery, please realize that I didn't make this system up. Who did? Benjamin Franklin. In his book, *The Autobiography of Benjamin Franklin,* Ben spends fifteen pages explaining how giving a week's strict attention to mastering one self-improvement topic before moving on to the next topic changed his life. Frank Bettger credits this system with his success too. Please note: spend *at least four months on these 4 topics.* Other topics might include: organization, knowledge of your business, listening, and closing.

Again: Why Use a Poor Man's Computer and/or a Training Computer?

You also do this to arm your self-worth and self-respect. Because the things you say to yourself are just as important as what you say to others.

Negative people practice being negative. They're like misers who take out all their bad thoughts and count them every night.

If a mother constantly tells her son that he's an idiot, he's eventually going to believe it. The words reiterate in his mind and compound like money in a billionaire's bank account. Some of us have had to live through experiences like that, or even worse nightmares, and the only way to conquer it is to tell yourself, "I'm going to show you something. I am good enough. I am 110% better than you. I have pride. I am intelligent. I am dedicated. I do things the right way no matter how tempted I may be to do the wrong thing."

Booker T. Washington once said: "I have learned that success is to be measured not so much by the position that one has reached in life as by the obstacles which he has overcome while trying to succeed."

Keep that in mind the next time you think you've had a rough day. Think about the obstacles that Booker T. Washington or Jackie Robinson were able to overcome. How did they do it? They had a powerful sense of pride and they wouldn't get down on themselves. Positive self-talk compounds just as quickly as the negative.

You Are Important!

Imagine that you are attending a funeral. There is a large crowd of people gathered near the long, closed casket, and as you strain curiously to see the inscription on the headstone, you discover that your name is there.

Glancing at the faces of the mourners, you recognize them as buyers and sellers that you had helped during your career. You never suspected that all these people cared about you. You might ask yourself, Why are all these people here? Why? Because you, my friend, made a difference in their lives.

Not me, you say, I'm just a buyer's agent. They'll forget all about me in two months. Not true.

Realize that when you sell a home and keep in touch with your clients, you become more than just an agent. You become a person of honor: a hall-of-famer in that household.

Along this line, here's a story from my personal experience. My mother worked in real estate for many years, and after she had died, I was given the task of writing her obituary. The local newspaper was supposed to publish the article on a Friday, and her funeral was taking place the following day, Saturday, so I anticipated that the church would be overflowing with people. Instead it was about half-full. One of my sisters met me in the parking lot and told me that the newspaper had failed to publish the article. She had discovered the mistake earlier and had forgotten to tell me. She had called everybody she knew and half of them had showed up.

I felt kind of sad about it. My mother had worked hard in real estate for 30 years and had been friends with a lot of people. If we could postpone the funeral for a week, I thought, then everybody could read about it in the newspaper, and.. Right.

Dream about it. Funerals don't get postponed.

Once inside the church, my wife asked if I could go to the van to fetch some tissues, and I remember walking outside to the empty parking lot, feeling sad and kind of sorry for my mother.

Then the strangest thing happened. This mad-dash horde of real estate people descended upon the place. It reminded me of a caravan of hungry real estate agents who are swarming onto a broker open luncheon at noon on a Friday caravan. Apparently the real estate agents who had worked with her over the years had found out about the newspaper mix-up earlier and had spread the word. They'd posted a message on the MLS computer bulletin board and had contacted people who they knew she had worked with. It was funny because in less than fifteen minutes a church that had been about half-full suddenly became crowded. People were standing in the back vestibule. I couldn't believe it. And as I reentered the church and walked up the aisle, I noticed several strangely familiar faces. People were there who I hadn't seen in years. I saw faces of buyers who my mother had helped to purchase homes. Real estate agents who I thought were too busy for little people. It reminded me of the last scene of *It's a Wonderful Life* when George Bailey realizes that the entire town of Bedford Falls has been affected by his life in some way.

My mother had made a difference.

I mention this story because most of us don't ever consider that to many of our buyers and sellers, even to other agents, we are heroes.

Why?

Because we are one-sided and only want to make money? No. Because we are all people. And when you manage to help collect two parties and bring them together for their mutual good, you've done your job. People pat you on the back. Over time we forget about it.

What will people say about you?

I think that most people will agree that you are making a surprising difference in their lives. They see you as being an important person, so why not accept this intelligent assessment? In fact, why not pick up a pen and print your name above the phrase, "the person who made a difference." This is what your headstone might look like:

<u>   Mary Logian   </u>
The person who made a difference

Surprisingly, your life does make a difference! Your thoughts and actions are important. Your life has a purpose. Please don't forget this!

Too many of us pack a lot of garbage in our heads. We get afraid of things. We get down on ourselves, punishing ourselves if we're not perfect. But it's not really what happens to us that counts, it's the way our minds look at it.

I want you to realize that you are somebody important. Accept yourself. Be proud of who you are! Did you know that there are people you're going to meet who are going to be glad that they met you? Not everybody, but you know what I mean. The Santiago family was living next to a neighbor who used to curse at their children, and you rescued them from that situation before it turned violent. You were the agent who turned renters into homeowners. Other agents told the Johnson family that their bankruptcy wouldn't allow them to purchase but you tried anyway and managed to get them into a house. If it weren't for you, Wendy Smith would never have been able to sell that condo. She appreciates you as do the Johnsons and Santiagos.

So do other agents.

If you're in a slump, call up a past client today. Stop by with some cookies for their kids. You might be surprised at how much the children have grown, and how much they still remember you!

How much they care about you.

There is a reason that you passed your real estate exam. There is a reason that you made it, and countless others failed the test. You are unique. You have a purpose in your career: a mission. Look again at the mission statement you wrote at my prompting earlier in this chapter. Remember your mission.

The Bible says you have to ask in order to receive, so why not give somebody new or old a call, just to let them know that you were thinking about them. Ask them if they know of anybody you can help. You might be surprised!

A Documented Study for the Doubting Thomas

Some of you might be thinking that I'm dwelling too much on the subject of attitude. One real estate agent sniffed and said, "This is that same old Notre Dame halftime locker room crap about having a positive attitude. I've heard this stuff a million times before!"

Maybe you have heard it before, but consider this. A Harvard Business School study on sales determined that there are four factors critical to success in sales: (1) information, (2) intelligence, (3) skill and (4) attitude.

What is most interesting is that all the factors were ranked by importance. Intelligence, skill and information received quite a remarkable score. Out of a possible 100%, the three of them received a combined total of 7%.

Attitude, having enthusiasm and a pleasant manner, was awarded a whopping 93% mark. Think about that. **93%!** Which means if you get nothing else out of this book, realize the vital importance of your attitude.

It's funny but new people and part-time agents are often so lucky! Many of them show the worst possible homes but because of their cheerful, happy-go-lucky attitudes they manage to dodge a bullet, hang in and make the sale! Right? I've seen it happen again and again. An excited, new, part-time agent with no skill, product information or intelligence beats a grumpy, intelligent, full-time professional with years of experience. Why? Two words: great attitude! These new agents smile and laugh and try hard to be the best buyer's agents around and guess what happens? *They fake it and they make it.* People love them. It's like the saying of Mr. Walter P. Chrysler who wrote **"More than enthusiasm. I would say excitement. I like to see men get excited. When they get excited, they get customers excited, and we get business."**

Your attitude shines through in everything you do.

Keep your attitude up, won't you?

CHAPTER TWENTY
Final Thoughts

I started out this book by telling you why I wrote it. A major reason was that I didn't like some of the practices and notions that I saw around me in the real estate business. I wanted to inspire real estate people to make sales by doing the right thing. I also wanted to show new people and part-time agents that they could use imagination and creativity to solve their sales challenges. Here's a story that illustrates how I think you can take the ideas from this book to become a surprisingly better agent.

There was once an auto mechanic who was trying to mount a front grille on a truck. But no matter how hard he tried, he couldn't get the grille to fit. Looking around the auto yard he suddenly noticed that there were five other trucks that had been taken apart, so he assumed that the grille must have come from another vehicle. That's why it didn't fit!

When the shop manager stopped by, the mechanic asked for his advice. The shop manager examined the grille and said: "No, I'm certain that this grille belongs on this truck. In fact I'd be willing to bet $200 on it."

Armed with this new information and an attitude that he would be able to fix the truck, the mechanic turned the grille in a slightly different position, and soon found the correct solution. The grille fit perfectly.

The point of this story is that as soon as the mechanic knew that there was a solution, he discovered a way to fix the truck. As soon as he changed his attitude, he found a way to do something that before he had thought was impossible.

In selling real estate, we agents constantly face challenges. We have days where nothing seems to go right. Yet we're rarely told that the surprising thing that separates a champion salesperson from an ordinary salesperson, is that the champion thinks flexibly. He or she uses imagination, creativity and energy to solve a problem, along with his or her individual talents. He or she doesn't just learn a closing technique. The champion agent will take a new idea and then figure out how to make it meaningful to his or her life.

I can't wait to
get started!

One agent, for example, told me that after reading this book he managed to take two listings. He said that after passing out a newsletter in a neighborhood, he used a farm package provided by a title company to telephone-canvas all the owners. Now, did it bother me that he used my ideas on *sellers* instead of buyers? Of course not.

I'm convinced that many of us in sales look for reasons why things *won't* work for us. There are agents who will start reading this book and will put it down because they know that things won't be the same for them. But instead of looking around for a reason why something *won't* work, why not change your way of thinking and find a way to get it done?

Why not concentrate on 10 ideas in this book that might work for you, instead of focusing on the two that might not? Then spend one week on each new idea. Your chances of success with your clients will be greater if you do!

I started this book talking about an experience I had with a young top agent who had two choices: to keep a promise and do the right thing, or to break a promise and put a few more bucks in his pocket. And I think that a situation like this might come up in your life sometime. I know it has in mine more than once.

Sometimes it's just a decision to follow your conscience or not follow it. But if you do follow your conscience, you have to let the chips fall where they may. Have faith that things will work out for the best. They usually do, don't you agree?

Hey, even the IRS was nice to me, can you believe that?

About nine months from when they relieved my bank account of its funds, the Internal Revenue Service sent my money back to me with interest! Incredible, isn't it?

I guess what I'm saying is that **the secret to this business is to do the best you can**. When you get kicked in the head, you lick your wounds and dry your tears. Then you get up, learn from your mistakes and keep on going. You do the right thing even when you're sorely tempted to do the wrong thing. If you can do the right thing enough times, word-of-mouth advertising begins to buzz through town. And even if you're as dumb as a stump, people will talk about you and will want to meet you, or send you referrals. Even if you don't have as many listings as the top agent in town.

You'll probably have competitors scratching their heads, saying, "I don't get it. Why do people like to do business with that guy or girl? He doesn't advertise as much as me. What does he or she have that I don't?"

Some people might say that they like you better. Others will say that you have a knack for finding the best homes in town. Some will even say that you're the best agent they've ever met!

But I think the real secret is that you have become a surprisingly better real estate agent. You have the courage to triumph over the meanness and selfishness that seem to be prevalent in real estate these days. You accept responsibility for the consequences of your actions and decisions that you have made based on ethical as well as practical considerations. You may not become as famous as some agents or make more money than others, but I think you'll be selling homes to buyers the right way. It's not always the easiest way, but in the long run it's the best way, don't you agree? (Say yes.)

Reading & Listening Resources

Helpful Reading Material

How to Win Friends and Influence People Dale Carnegie

How to Master the Art of Selling Real Estate Tom Hopkins

The Magic of Thinking Big David J. Schwartz

How to Develop a Six-Figure Income in Real Estate: Superstar Selling the Mike Ferry Way Mike Ferry

How to List & Sell Residential Real Estate Successfully Barb Schwarz

The One Minute Salesperson Spencer Johnson, M.D. with Larry Wilson.

Closing Techniques Stephan Schiffman

When Anger Hurts: Quieting the Storm Within Matthew McKay, Judith McKay, Kirk Johnson, Peter D. Rogers

Real Estate as a Second Language Roger Reitzel Illustrated by David J. Schutten

See You at the Top Zig Ziglar

The Greatest Salesman in the World Og Mandino

Dig Your Well Before You're Thirsty: The Only Networking Book You'll Ever Need Harvey Mackay.

How to List and Sell Real Estate in the 90's Danielle Kennedy, Warren Jamison

Think and Grow Rich Napoleon Hill

How to Close Every Sale Joe Girard and Robert L. Shook

How to Sell Anything to Anybody Joe Girard, Stanley H. Brown

Helpful Listening Material

Mission Accomplished! The Power to Achieve Bob Davies

Turning Point Live Brian Buffini and Tim Templeton

The Legends of Real Estate Jim Droz

Floyd Wickman & The Sweathog Program Floyd Wickman

Selling Strategies & Techniques & Procedures Mike Domer

Can't find these titles? Try using the Internet! Point and click to these web sites:

www.amazon.com or **www.barnesandnoble.com**

Counter Offer Comparison Sheet

Seller's Original Terms	Buyer's Purchase Agreement	Seller's Counter Offer
Price	Price:	Price:
Down pmt:	Down pmt:	Down pmt:
*Monthly pmt:	*Monthly pmt:	*Monthly pmt:
COE date:	date:	COE date:
FHA non-allowables:	non-allowables:	FHA non-allowables:
Discount points	Discount points	Discount points
Buyers' Costs:	Buyers' Costs:	Buyers' Costs:
Repairs	Repairs	Repairs
Home Warranty:	Home Warranty:	Home Warranty:
Escrow co.	Escrow co.	Escrow co.
Title co:	Title co:	Title co:
Loan commitment:	Loan commitment:	Loan commitment:
Inspection time:	Inspection time:	Inspection time:
Misc:	Misc:	Misc:

Notes Page

GLOSSARY

Annual Percentage Rate (APR)

Everything financed in a mortgage loan (interest, loan fees, points or other charges) and expressed as a percentage of the loan amount. (Note: the APR is usually slightly above the actual interest rate alone).

Closing Costs

Costs the buyer must pay at the time of closing in addition to the down payment: including points, mortgage insurance premium, fire insurance, prepayments for property taxes, etc.

Contingency

A condition put on an offer to buy a home dependent upon something else; such as the prospective buyer purchasing the home contingent upon obtaining financing. Possible, but not certain to happen.

Conventional Mortgage

A customary type of mortgage not insured by either the Federal Housing Administration (FHA) or the Dept. of Veteran's Affairs (VA), usually requiring a down payment of 5%, 10%, 20% and/or private mortgage insurance (pmi).

Earnest Money

Funds submitted with a purchase contract to show a serious intention to follow through with the purchase. Earnest money is placed by the broker into escrow where it becomes part of the down payment or closing costs.

Escrow

A procedure or legal contract in which documents or transfers of cash and property are put in the care of a third party, other than the buyer or seller, and kept there until the terms of the contract are fulfilled. Escrow is considered closed when title is recorded in the new buyer's name.

Fair Housing Act

A Federal law that prohibits housing discrimination based on race, color, national origin, religion, sex, family status or disability.

Fannie Mae

Fannie Mae is a government funded corporation that increases the supply of money that mortgage lenders can make available to homebuyers by purchasing loans in the secondary mortgage market. Fannie Mae is also accountable to a board of directors and shareholders.

The FHA

The Federal Housing Administration arranges financing for a loan which will be insured against loss by the U.S. Dept. of Housing and Urban Development aka: HUD. FHA financing normally requires a 3% minimum down payment and a lump sum mortgage insurance that is added directly to the loan amount.

Freddie Mac

A stockholder-owned corporation chartered by congress to increase the supply of money that mortgage lenders can make available to homebuyers, but the government has no ownership interest in the company. Freddie Mac is accountable to a board of directors and to its shareholders. In the event of borrower default, Freddie Mac acquires properties through foreclosure.

Homeowner's Insurance

Insurance that protects the homeowner from "casualty" losses (damage to the home or personal property) and from "liability" damages to other people or property. Required by lenders prior to funding a home loan.

HUD Repo's

Homes repossessed by the Dept. of Housing and Urban development and sold by sealed bid or open auction to qualified purchasers. Also known as HUD homes.

Loan Origination Fee

A fee charged by a lender for evaluating, preparing and submitting a proposed mortgage loan.

Mortgage Insurance Premium (MIP)

A charge paid by a borrower in order to secure financing by a conventional lender, usually when making a down payment of less than 20% of the purchase price.

Point

An amount equal to 1% of the principal loan amount being borrowed. The lender may charge a borrower one or more "points" in order to provide the loan.

Property Taxes

Taxes which are based on the assessed value of the home and paid by the homeowner in order to provide community services such as schools, public works and other costs of local government. Usually due twice a year or paid as a part of the monthly mortgage payment in FHA and VA loans.

Title Insurance

Protects lenders and homeowners against loss of their interest in a property due to legal defects in the title.

VA Loan

A loan guaranteed by the Department of Veterans Affairs against loss for the lender. Loans of zero down payment are made for eligible past and present members of the armed forces.

VA Repo's

Homes repossessed by the Dept. of Veterans Affairs and sold by auction to qualified purchasers. Note: purchasers do not have to be veterans in order to purchase these homes or obtain zero down financing from the Dept. of Veteran's Affairs.

Index

Selling Homes 1-2-3

Chapter One

What Is Techno-Selling?

When I first started out in real estate, I was showing homes to a single mom who brought along her three children to look at houses. This was not a very good idea because these three children were not well behaved. They would fight, touch things, eat candy that didn't belong to them, and play with other children's toys. What would their mother do? Nothing. She pretended not to notice. It was like she was thinking, "I am too busy purchasing a home to watch my children." So guess who ended up telling the children to put the toys back where they found them? That's right. Me. Yours truly.

One time, we arrived at a home and taped to the front door was a sign that read: "Do not let the cat outside."

When I opened the door, I immediately began to worry. This cat looked like a runner. Magnificent in his white coat with tan and gray spots, he meowed something softly to me as I walked past him. When I think back to this incident, I realize his "meow" probably meant something like, "Good luck trying to catch me, dude."

I had a feeling that one of the children was going to let the cat out, so I showed the home quickly. Finally, when all of the children had left the house and were safely walking down the sidewalk to my car with their mother, I closed the front door to the house and breathed a sigh of relief. Whew!

Do You Want to Make More Sales?

Read Bob's new book, *Techno-Selling*! What if James Bond was a salesperson? Think he might use technology to help him sell?

In *Techno-Selling* you will learn quick and easy techno tips:
· How to build a Free Online Sales Office.

· How to convert signed contracts to e-mails without using a scanner!

· How to keep your name stuck inside your client's computer.

What people on the Internet are saying about *Techno-Selling:*

· "I haven't laughed this hard since Seinfeld."

· "Readers will smile all the way through."

· "Techno- selling is a funny, informative and yet inspirational book."

· "I loved this book and I'm not in sales."

To purchase a copy of Techno-Selling, visit the Web site at:
www.techno-selling.com
Also, are you are interested in reading about Real Estate Horror
Stories? Read Bob's new book "*Real Estate Horror Stories*"
www.realestatehorror.com
Both books are available at any regular or online bookstore!